CW00343986

SOUTHERN
SHEDS in CAMERA

Plate 1: It is a hot day in 1929, and ex-South Eastern Railway Class R 0-6-0T No. A336 pauses briefly before leaving Folkestone Junction shed, while the driver finishes a refreshing cup of tea.

G. Coltas

SOUTHERN
SHEDS in CAMERA

Roger Griffiths

Oxford Publishing Co.

Dedication

For Carl and Simon

A FOULIS-OPC Railway Book

© 1989 R. Griffiths & Haynes Publishing Group

All rights reserved. No part of this book may be reproduced or transmitted in any form or by any means, electronic or mechanical, including photocopying, recording or by any information storage or retrieval systems, without written permission from the copyright owner.

Published by:
Haynes Publishing Group
Sparkford, Near Yeovil, Somerset. BA22 7JJ

Haynes Publications Inc.
861 Lawrence Drive, Newbury Park, California 91320, USA.

Printed by J.H. Haynes & Co.

British Library Cataloguing in Publication Data

Griffiths, Roger
 Southern sheds in camera.
 1. Southern England. Railway services. Southern
 Railway Company. Locomotive depots, history
 I. Title
 385'.314

ISBN 0-86093-415 2

Library of Congress Catalog Card Number
 89-84302

Publisher's note: A number of the photographs in this album are from original prints of poor quality, but have been included because of their rarity, historical interest and importance.

Plate 2: Faversham shed c1936.   *W.A. Camwell*

Introduction

The saying goes: "variety is the spice of life". So it was with the steam engine sheds of the Southern Railway and its forebears, in a period of development that covered at least 115 years and involved well over 200 buildings.

Which Southern constituent had the honour of building the first shed is debatable – the 1830 Canterbury & Whitstable Railway (later SER), was initially cable-worked, but the famous 0-4-0 *Invicta* was operated over a short stretch of line, so was she housed in a shed? The answer is not certain. Next, in 1834, came the remote Bodmin & Wadebridge Railway (LSWR), which definitely did have a shed at Wadebridge and possibly at Bodmin. Two years later, another SER constituent, the London & Greenwich Railway, opened its Deptford locomotive depot, but it would be yet another two years before the first 'major' company's sheds opened. Those were of the London & Southampton Railway (LSWR), at Nine Elms and Woking, being followed in 1839 by the first LBSCR constituents' depots at New Cross and Croydon (London & Croydon Railway), and in 1840 at Brighton (London & Brighton Railway).

After that, things moved apace, riding high on the 'Railway Mania', with nearly 40 sheds being put up in the 1840s, mostly in the last three years of that decade. The 1850s were somewhat quieter, following the financial crises brought about by the 'Mania'. Only a handful of sheds appeared up to 1855, but from then until the late 1860s came another surge, with over 50 new building locations and one or two first replacements. 1858 saw the first LCDR depot, at Faversham, followed by six more, up to 1865, as that company's operations expanded. In doing so the opening shots were fired in the LCDR's Kentish 'war' with the SER, that was to prove so destructive to both railways' fortunes. 1862 was the year of the first shed on the Isle of Wight, with eventually eleven being operated by the individualistic railway companies of the island.

1870-1889 was more a period of consolidation, some 33 new depots coming into use – seven in 1874 alone – with an increasing incidence of second generation buildings at a number of locations. However, it was the 1890s and particularly the 1900s that witnessed numerous replacement sheds, petering out in the last four years prior to World War One, with no further development in that decade. Came the 1920s and it was left to the LSWR to add the last two pre-Grouping engine sheds, after which it was 1927 before the Southern Railway embarked upon a programme of 14 sheds, in the years up to 1937. Which leaves the period to Nationalisation and beyond and provision by British Railways of its solitary new steam locomotive shed on the Southern Region, a departmental depot at Meldon Quarry.

Regarding construction materials, brick-built sheds saw by far the most widespread application, greatly outnumbering the total of buildings made in stone, wood, concrete and corrugated asbestos and iron. Roofs were almost universally of the pitched pattern, with gable or hipped ends. Transverse pitches, and most especially the maintenance intensive northlight roof, saw far less use among the Southern's constituents than in any other part of the country. Again, unlike their northern and western neighbours, the southern companies rarely used the roundhouse shed. The LBSCR was the most prolific employer, starting with the 'Octagon' and 'Rooter' buildings at New Cross, culminating in the triple round sheds at Battersea Park, and continuing with small part-buildings at Eastbourne and Horsham. Two part-round sheds were seen on the LSWR, at Nine Elms and Guildford, while the LCDR used the same pattern for its sole example, at Longhedge. SER claims to a 'roundhouse' were limited to a small turntable building at Cannon Street, which leaves another solitary representative, the only square plan-form turntable shed, at Fratton, an LBSCR/LSWR joint building.

Some measure of standardisation of its straight sheds was applied quite early by the LBSCR, with small two-road, two-engine buildings being provided at most major stations and junctions. That appears to have been in line with the thinking of the company's then engineer, Craven, who chose to design his engines to suit particular services and therefore limit them to fixed locations. But, when Stroudley took over, there came the change whereby he greatly standardised LBSCR locomotive stock, allowing closure of most of the small sheds. That was at a very early time – the beginning of the 1870s.

Elsewhere, standardisation was generally lacking, except on the LSWR from 1885, when that company employed its glass-gabled roofs for the first time. That was at Nine Elms, the LSWR expanding upon the theme with six other large sheds in the years up to 1908. About the LCDR and SER, only a few specific comments may be made. Namely, both companies greatly favoured old-fashioned devices like decorative brickwork and arched entrances and because of their costly rivalry, each did less than their neighbours by way of expanding or modernising engine shed facilities.

In fact, none of the constituents were totally forward-looking, except the LSWR in its very last years, employing such things as mechanical coaling plants and suchlike. The LBSCR was, for want of a better word, 'forced' into installing water softening plants at a very early stage, because of the nature of the groundwater in chalky southern England. But overall, LBSCR sheds were cramped and employed primitive coaling and repair facilities, and little thought was spared for even the most basic amenities for the men employed in them.

Things changed under the Southern Railway, which wholeheartedly adopted the concrete medium for practically everything, but particularly engine sheds, from a legacy of 'last-ditch' thinking by the LSWR. Indeed, for a railway company with its sights set firmly on electrification, the SR's steam shed programme was quite amazing in its scope and followed from the very realistic attitude – for the time – that steam power would be around for quite a while. Six large new engine sheds were built between 1928 and 1935, all of them employing northlight roofs, a design which was a much better maintenance prospect when formed of concrete. Eight small depots were built during roughly the same period, but not all were made in concrete, with corrugated sheeting, brick, and even wood being used.

In a manner that appears contrary with its forward

thinking, the SR did not universally employ mechanical coaling plants at its big new depots. This followed from experience with the first two coalers, LSWR-inspired, at Nine Elms and Feltham, and the SR's first, at Exmouth Junction, where the friable Welsh coal did not stand up well to the rough, bulk handling it received. Two later coaling plants were put up by the SR though, at Ramsgate and Stewarts Lane, but they were supplied with less fragile fuels – Yorkshire Hards and Kentish respectively; it is believed the former also became the norm at Nine Elms and Feltham.

Thus did British Railways inherit a veritable mixture, with engine sheds ranging from the positively archaic and/or decrepit, to installations that were as efficient as a steam locomotive depot could be. Apart from the small shed at Meldon, BR built no new depots for the Southern Region, but did undertake an almost immediate widespread programme of re-roofings and partial rebuildings, that lasted until the latter half of the 'fifties. By that time, steam's death knell had sounded, so further investment was kept strictly to a minimum. Even so, for the railway that was frequently the most modern thinking when it came to motive power, and

always had the smallest number of steam locomotives of the "Big Four", to the Southern went the honour of running the last steam main line in the south of Britain. Bulleid's Pacifics and some BR Standards went out in a blaze of glory on 9th July 1967, the last eight steam sheds going with them.

Early rationalisation of the shoal of small depots around south London, and closure due to pioneering electrification schemes, ensured that a surprising number of SR and constituents' steam sheds were re-employed, and may still be seen today. At least ten – wholly or in part – are still serving BR, as electric multiple unit depots, or in some other use, and perhaps another dozen are in private occupation. In addition, there are the sizeable but sad remains of Ashford depot, and at Tunbridge Wells West, the still intact building's fate hangs in the balance of a projected preservation scheme. Go and visit one – or all – close your eyes, and imagine what it *really* used to be like!

Roger Griffiths
Doha, Qatar.

Southern Railway System Maps

The following maps show, with a few insignificant exceptions, the full extent of the rail systems of the Southern Railway and its constituent companies. Further detailed are a number of minor and light railways which, by sometimes outrageous use of "author's licence", have had their locomotive sheds included in this book. All told, some 230 depots are indicated, many of which saw their demise long before the Southern Railway came into existence. Also counted

are those "official" depots where no shed building seems to have been provided, or in a couple of cases, where a building was indeed put up, but whose actual use by locomotives seems unlikely. Then came a few sheds whose entire existences must be considered dubious. It is a fact to say that these lists are *not* definitive – further sheds were being discovered right up to this book's closure for printing – more have yet to be found!

Locomotive Sheds of the Southern Railway and its Constituents

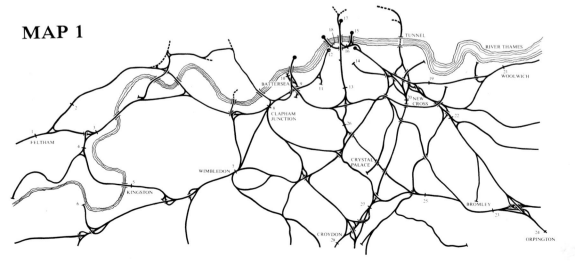

MAP 1

Map 1 London Area

1 Feltham
2 Hounslow (no building)
3 Twickenham
4 Strawberry Hill (Fulwell)
5 Kingston (upon Thames)
6 Hampton Court (2 sheds)
7 Wimbledon P.W. Depot
8 Clapham Junction
9 Longhedge (also known as Battersea and Stewarts Lane – 2 sheds)
10 Battersea Park (2 sheds)
11 Nine Elms (3 sheds)
12 Waterloo
13 Camberwell (New Road) (obscure)
14 Bricklayers Arms
15 Cannon Street
16 Ewer Street (no building)
17 Holborn Viaduct
18 Charing Cross (Belvedere Road)
19 Deptford
20 New Cross
21 Woolwich Arsenal
22 Hither Green
23 Bickley
24 Orpington
25 Beckenham (Junction)
26 Herne Hill
27 Norwood Junction
28 West Croydon

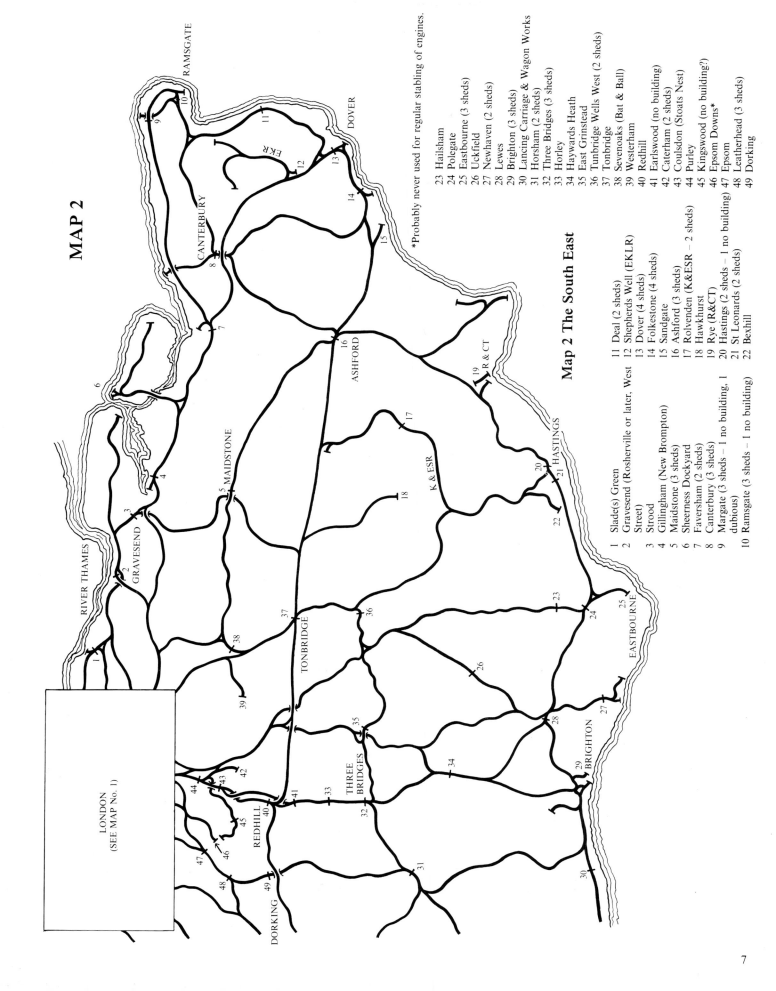

MAP 2

Map 2 The South East

1 Slade(s) Green
2 Gravesend (Rosherville or later, West Street)
3 Strood
4 Gillingham (New Brompton)
5 Maidstone (3 sheds)
6 Sheerness Dockyard
7 Faversham (2 sheds)
8 Canterbury (3 sheds)
9 Margate (3 sheds – 1 no building, 1 dubious)
10 Ramsgate (3 sheds – 1 no building)
11 Deal (2 sheds)
12 Shepherds Well (EKLR)
13 Dover (4 sheds)
14 Folkestone (4 sheds)
15 Sandgate
16 Ashford (3 sheds)
17 Rolvenden (K&ESR – 2 sheds)
18 Hawkhurst
19 Rye (R&CT)
20 Hastings (2 sheds – 1 no building)
21 St Leonards (2 sheds)
22 Bexhill
23 Hailsham
24 Polegate
25 Eastbourne (3 sheds)
26 Uckfield
27 Newhaven (2 sheds)
28 Lewes
29 Brighton (3 sheds)
30 Lancing Carriage & Wagon Works
31 Horsham (2 sheds)
32 Three Bridges (3 sheds)
33 Horley
34 Haywards Heath
35 East Grinstead
36 Tunbridge Wells West (2 sheds)
37 Tonbridge
38 Sevenoaks (Bat & Ball)
39 Westerham
40 Redhill
41 Earlswood (no building)
42 Caterham (2 sheds)
43 Coulsdon (Stoats Nest)
44 Purley
45 Kingswood (no building?)
46 Epsom Downs*
47 Epsom
48 Leatherhead (3 sheds)
49 Dorking

*Probably never used for regular stabling of engines.

LONDON (SEE MAP No. 1)

7

Map 3 The South

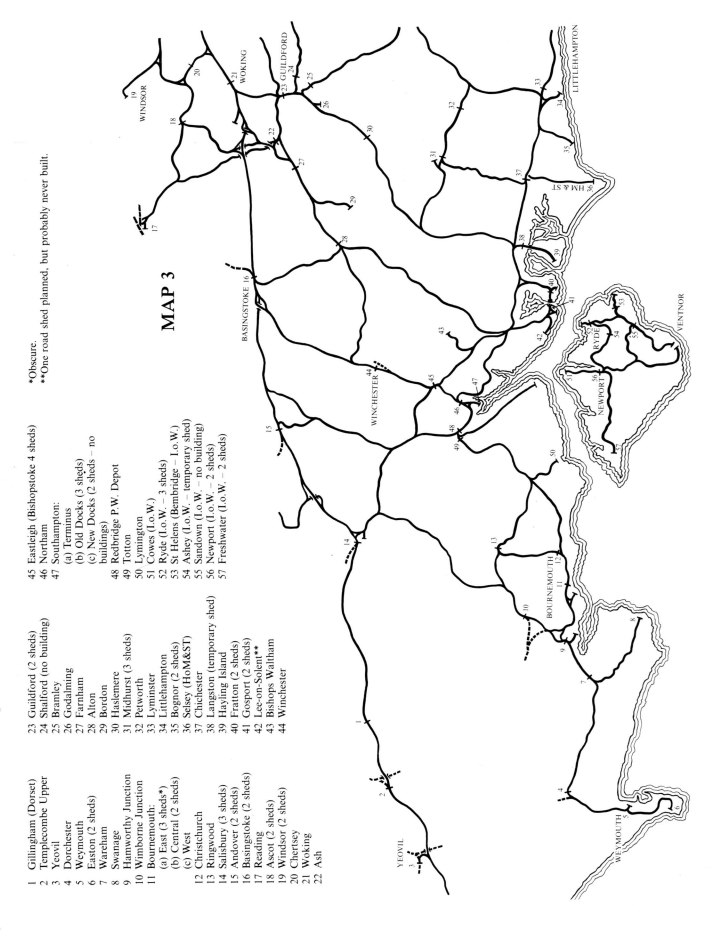

1 Gillingham (Dorset)
2 Templecombe Upper
3 Yeovil
4 Dorchester
5 Weymouth
6 Easton (2 sheds)
7 Wareham
8 Swanage
9 Hamworthy Junction
10 Wimborne Junction
11 Bournemouth:
　(a) East (3 sheds*)
　(b) Central (2 sheds)
　(c) West
12 Christchurch
13 Ringwood
14 Salisbury (3 sheds)
15 Andover (2 sheds)
16 Basingstoke (2 sheds)
17 Reading
18 Ascot (2 sheds)
19 Windsor (2 sheds)
20 Chertsey
21 Woking
22 Ash

23 Guildford (2 sheds)
24 Shalford (no building)
25 Bramley
26 Godalming
27 Farnham
28 Alton
29 Bordon
30 Haslemere
31 Midhurst (3 sheds)
32 Petworth
33 Lyminster
34 Littlehampton
35 Bognor (2 sheds)
36 Selsey (HoM&ST)
37 Chichester
38 Langston (temporary shed)
39 Hayling Island
40 Fratton (2 sheds)
41 Gosport (2 sheds)
42 Lee-on-Solent**
43 Bishops Waltham
44 Winchester

45 Eastleigh (Bishopstoke 4 sheds)
46 Northam
47 Southampton:
　(a) Terminus
　(b) Old Docks (3 sheds)
　(c) New Docks (2 sheds – no buildings)
48 Redbridge P.W. Depot
49 Totton
50 Lymington
51 Cowes (I.o.W.)
52 Ryde (I.o.W. – 3 sheds)
53 St Helens (Bembridge – I.o.W.)
54 Ashey (I.o.W. – temporary shed)
55 Sandown (I.o.W. – no building)
56 Newport (I.o.W. – 2 sheds)
57 Freshwater (I.o.W. – 2 sheds)

*Obscure.
**One road shed planned, but probably never built.

MAP 4

Map 4 The South West

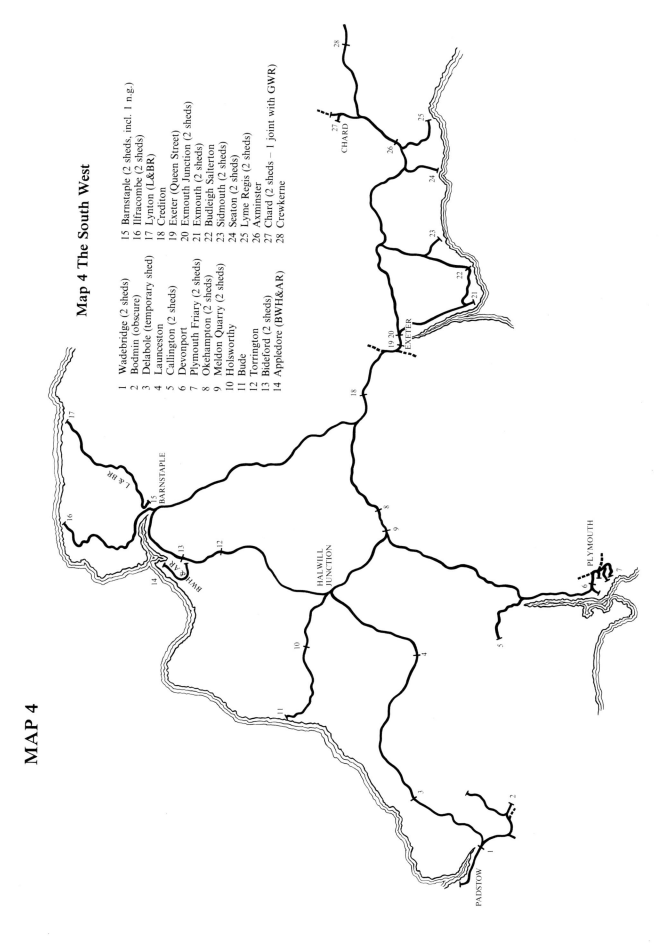

1	Wadebridge (2 sheds)	15	Barnstaple (2 sheds, incl. 1 n.g.)
2	Bodmin (obscure)	16	Ilfracombe (2 sheds)
3	Delabole (temporary shed)	17	Lynton (L&BR)
4	Launceston	18	Crediton
5	Callington (2 sheds)	19	Exeter (Queen Street)
6	Devonport	20	Exmouth Junction (2 sheds)
7	Plymouth Friary (2 sheds)	21	Exmouth (2 sheds)
8	Okehampton (2 sheds)	22	Budleigh Salterton
9	Meldon Quarry (2 sheds)	23	Sidmouth (2 sheds)
10	Holsworthy	24	Seaton (2 sheds)
11	Bude	25	Lyme Regis (2 sheds)
12	Torrington	26	Axminster
13	Bideford (2 sheds)	27	Chard (2 sheds – 1 joint with GWR)
14	Appledore (BWH&AR)	28	Crewkerne

The Sheds

Author's Note: This work follows the format of the author's other publication in this OPC series, *GWR Sheds in Camera,* in detailing sheds in alphabetical order. Ancillary facilities, breakdown cranes, etc, are included as appropriate, with some depots being covered in depth, in special "Focus" sections. As alluded to earlier, a considerable number of Southern constituent companies' engine sheds were closed very early on so, in consequence, their depiction in photographs is rare. Some did manage to 'creep in' to pictures though, usually by accident, and often in only a partial way. A number of such prints are shown in this volume and the author apologises for possible shortcomings in the quality and content of some, feeling that scarcity value alone merited their inclusion. All told, the book contains 318 photographs, covering some 145 locations and over 160 different buildings, and it is hoped that overall, they will be adequate recompense for any deficiences.

Plate 3: **Andover's** first LSWR shed was a single road affair opened in 1854 and sited roughly where the wagons may be seen in the photograph's far right distance. It was a singularly unlucky building, first being heavily damaged by a boiler explosion in 1856, then totally destroyed by fire in 1899! The two-road replacement shed, visible here at left in a picture dated 30th April 1928, was not opened until 1904. It joined a depot built in 1882/3 by the LSWR, for the SM&AR – later to become the MSWJR, then GWR. As may be seen, separate coaling facilities were provided for each company, a situation perpetuated, amazingly, by British Railways Western and Southern Regions, but the turntable sited between the buildings always was shared. The Western Region building closed in 1958 (three years before the MSWJ route), followed by the Southern Region shed in June 1962; commercial development now covers both sites.

H.C. Casserley

Plate 4: **Ash** shed was built by the SER in 1856, to provide motive power for services between Aldershot and Guildford. The LSWR also stationed engines at the depot for workings to Farnham, Bagshot and Tongham, which meant that the little shed usually had an allocation of four or five locomotives. By 1938 though, when this picture was taken, and Class U No. 1613 paused with a Redhill–Reading train, Class M7 No. 110 and its motor train were sufficient for the remaining duties. Closure came around 1946/47, but the building stands today, in private use.

Lens of Sutton

Plate 5: A somewhat unnecessary line to **Ashford** was built by the LCDR, under the auspices of the Maidstone & Ashford Railway, opened on 1st July 1884. It seems engine facilities were not initially provided at the terminus, but after the 1st November 1891 opening of a connecting spur to the SER station, LCDR locomotives were serviced at the SER's shed – for appropriate charges of course. This arrangement was not tolerated for long, so in 1894 the LCDR opened its own two-road locomotive depot. It had a short working life, being shut from 1st January 1899, simultaneous with closure to passengers of the LCDR's station. The shed became part of a goods depot and stood for many years, as this 29th March 1970 picture shows. Note the LCDR's late use of such outdated features as arched doorways, and the building's cramped position between the station and footbridge. By early 1970 it was out of use and demolition occurred in the following year.

B.I. Fletcher

Plate 6: **Ashford's** four-road SER shed opened in the 1840s and formed part of the works complex. As such, it became increasingly cramped, particularly after Ashford LCDR depot closed and its engines and duties absorbed. This picture shows the western end of the shed about 1918, with a pair of Class F1 4-4-0s prominent. Some thirteen years later, the SER shed was replaced by a new Southern Railway-built depot.

Author's collection

Plate 7: **Ashford Works** had its own allocation of locomotives for many years – three engines being stationed there on 15th October 1898, for example, and a number of Class C 0-6-0s and USA 0-6-0Ts in Departmental use, right up to the end of steam in 1967. This view across Ashford Works yard was taken on 22nd September 1963 and the Departmental locomotives' servicing facilities can be seen clearly. Note the grounded coach body for use by engine crews with, behind, a coal stage and water tank. The building looking like an engine shed was, in fact, the works weigh house; engines were parked on the ex-SER shed's pit roads. The former site of the SER depot's turntable can just be discerned between the weigh house and a pile of sleepers to its left.

W.T. Stubbs collection

Plate 8: The SR's 1931 ten-road concrete-built depot brought much-needed relief to **Ashford's** men and locomotives. Its 32 years of use in the service of steam was strenuous, as may be appreciated from this picture dating from 19th September 1950. Then came a further five years housing diesel locomotives, so by closure in 1968 its condition was poor and partial demolition had already occurred. A period of limbo ensued, as the still-born Ashford Steam Centre, before further clearance reduced the building to a small portion of its former size. Those crumbling remains still stand today.

B. Hilton

Plate 9: The LSWR opened a shed at **Axminster** around 1860, for engines giving banking assistance over Honiton Summit. 2-4-0 *Locke* (ex-Engineer's Department No. 4) was stationed here in the late 1880s, and Class 460 4-4-0s Nos 0460 and 0472 during World War One, by which time the shed had long been demolished. However, coal and water facilities were maintained at the station for engines working the Lyme Regis branch, opened in 1903. Those basic amenities are seen here at the back of the branch bay platform about 1947. Note the large number of passengers – and their bicycles – a poignant reminder of those saner, motor car-less days, of not so long ago.

Author's collection

Plates 10 & 11: **Barnstaple** saw its first North Devon Railway & Dock Company trains on 1st August 1854, when the line between Crediton and Bideford opened. For the first year though, services over this broad gauge route were operated by the Bristol & Exeter Railway, before handing over to the contractor, Thomas Brassey, to continue. The LSWR assumed the workings in 1861, introduced standard gauge stock over a third rail on 2nd March 1863, absorbed the NDR&DC on 1st January 1865, and finally eradicated Brunel's gauge in April 1877. During all this, Barnstaple engine shed opened and this is seen in two photos, from the south, above, around 1930 and from the north, below, on 27th September 1961. The photographs raise interesting questions. Was that stone-built section with the filled-in archway an original engine shed? Was the wooden shed built in two portions, at varying dates, seemingly as indicated by the differing heights of its two parts? Whatever, the wooden structure survived an increasing decrepitude until September 1964, when closure came, soon to be followed by demolition.

A.B. Macleod collection/National Railway Museum & W.T. Stubbs collection

Plate 12: **Basingstoke's** first engine shed was a single-road affair, sited on the 'down' side, probably opened with the line from Winchfield, on 12th June 1839. In the only known photograph of the depot, it is partly seen about 1890, with Beattie 'Volcano' Class 2-4-0 No. 26 (ex-*Gazelle*) standing alongside. This locomotive was withdrawn in September 1894.

S.C. Nash collection

Plate 13: By the end of the 19th century **Basingstoke's** first shed was no longer adequate so a replacement three-road depot was opened in 1905, this time situated on the 'up' side. That shed is shown below, across the turntable, on 19th September 1963, with a typically mixed bag of engines to be seen. They include at least one ex-GWR 4-6-0 (left) – that railway's engines visited the depot daily, after the 1950 closure of their own shed in the town. On the right is Bulleid Pacific No. 34054 *Lord Beaverbrook*.

W.T. Stubbs collection

Plate 14: Here is **Basingstoke's** covered coaling stage on 8th October 1961. The crane-equipped edifice was provided as part of an improvement programme carried through during the Second World War. Quite what the ex-GWR pannier tank was doing, so far from her home at Goodwick, West Wales, is not clear, but doubtless the trainspotters of Basingstoke made a good "cop" that day!

T. Wright

Plate 15: **Basingstoke** shed survived until the end of steam over the Waterloo-Weymouth route, finally closing on 9th July 1967. Demolition occurred within two years as BR methodically went about its task of eradicating the legacy of 130 years of history; this sad photograph was taken as the wreckers paused in their act of destruction.

Dr. T.A. Gough

Plate 16: The LBSCR's major locomotive depot at **Battersea Park** had its origins in the West End of London & Crystal Palace Railway, which opened its line, and a three-road engine shed on 29th March 1858, only to be absorbed by the LBSCR from 1st July 1859. Over the next 30 years, increasing traffic caused the Brighton company to add three roundhouses, immediately adjacent to the viaduct north of Battersea Park station. Two on the 'up' side appeared in 1869 and 1889, while on the 'down' side the third was opened in 1870; meantime, the original straight shed was closed, in 1877. The three round sheds are seen to advantage (to the right of the three gasholders) in this aerial photograph dating from 1910. That such a picture should come from the very early years of flight is entirely due to the fact that the Battersea balloon ground was situated in the area of land between the gasholders and viaduct. Two balloon-manufacturing companies had their works in five arches of the viaduct – the *British* Wright Brothers, and Short Brothers, a famous name, still trading today. Aircraft too were built on this site, but had to be dragged through the streets to Wanstead Flats, the nearest available terrain offering airfield capabilities.

Royal Air Force Museum

Plate 17: Seen below are the entrances to the southerly (1889) **Battersea Park** shed around 1900, and it is evident from this print and *Plate 19* that the shed's original arched portals had not been too successful a design!

F. Burtt collection/NRM

Plate 18: The aerial photograph shows that the 'down' side (1870) round shed at **Battersea Park** had extensions added between its sides and the viaduct, creating a building that was triangular in planform. This allowed lengthening of some of the internal roads and installation of repair facilities, both features as evidenced by this superb interior photograph, dating from 30th April 1921. The famed LBSCR "bull" was still evident, even in those latter days of the company's existence. Note too, the small turntable – only 45ft, compared with 55 footers in the two 'up' side buildings.

H.C. Casserley

Plate 19: **Battersea Park's** 'up' side sheds are seen in this picture, showing the northernmost (1869) building as a backdrop to 'Gladstone' No. 192. The date was 17th May 1924, and No. 192 – formerly named *Jacomb-Hood* – had another $3\frac{1}{2}$ years life before withdrawal.

H.C. Casserley

Plate 20: Following closure to locomotive use, **Battersea Park** roundhouses saw many more years use as a goods depot, latterly for National Carriers, as may be seen from this June 1978 picture of the 'up' side. Note that the south shed has lost its roof – as had the 'down' building by that time. Since this picture was taken the vista has been transformed by a massive new commercial development, so these sheds are no more. The remains of the 'down' side structure served as a walled storage enclosure for a construction company until mostly demolished about April 1988.

Author

Plates 21 & 22: The Crowhurst, Sidley & Bexhill Railway was a fairly late addition, not being completed until 1st June 1902. Worked by the SECR, it was invariably the older classes of ex-SER locomotive that operated the line, based on a two-road shed at **Bexhill**. Motor trains took over services about 1936 and Bexhill depot closed a year later. Subsequent branch line power included diesels from 1958, until the demise of the entire line from 15th June 1964. Because of its generous proportions, relative to its duties, Bexhill depot was often used as a repository for redundant locomotives. This is evidenced by the upper picture, which dates from 1930, when stored B2X class No. 324 was posed for the photographer. Eventually though, even that duty ceased and the shed was adapted for private commercial use. As such it survives today, in excellent condition, as seen in the lower picture, which was taken from the south during the summer of 1987; the building now serves as a council depot.

S.C. Nash collection & S.C. Nash

Plate 23: First rails to **Bickley** arrived on 5th July 1858, from Bromley (Shortlands). The route to Rochester followed on 3rd December 1860 and it is thought Bickley shed was in existence by that time. The depot consisted of a single road building, but despite the small size it always sported a considerable allocation. For example, twelve Class R 0-4-4Ts, Nos 658-669, were transferred away when the depot closed in 1901, upon the inception of Orpington shed. The photograph dates from 1908 and the mostly demolished building is visible on the left hand side. On the right is just seen Bickley 'A' signal box, right of which again was a 44ft turntable and several more stabling sidings, where, apparently, engines were coaled from wagons.

Lens of Sutton

Plate 24: The North Devon Railway & Dock Company's history is detailed in the caption to *Plates 10 & 11.* The original northern terminus of the NDRDC was **Bideford,** where a single-road shed was erected immediately beyond the station platform end. This poor, but priceless print shows the shed and station, with broad gauge 2-4-0 *Creedy* and train. The period was about 1860, some twelve years before the line was extended to a new Bideford station, and on to Torrington, where a standard gauge shed was put up, allowing closure of the Bideford building. It is known that the latter still stood in 1886, but when final demolition occurred is a mystery; nowadays, the entire railway through Bideford is no more.

Author's collection

Plate 25: There was another railway which served Bideford, the short-lived Bideford, Westward Ho! & Appledore, a privately owned line that opened on 20th May 1901, only to be closed again, on 27th March 1917. There was a small, one-road shed at Appledore, brought into use on 1st May 1908, but the BWHA's main engine depot was at **Bideford.** That substantial three-road building saw many more years alternative service after closure and removal of the railway, and it is seen here, in July 1964, in use by a dairy company. Remember those blue milk-dispensing machines of pre-vandal times? Six old pennies bought you a carton of goodness – what does 2¹/2p get you today?

T.J. Edgington

Plate 26: Worked by the LSWR, the Bishops Waltham Railway opened on 1st June 1863, but it was 14 years before the operating company provided a one-road engine shed at the terminus. Class O2 No.217 was sub-shedded from Eastleigh in August 1911, while from the late 1920s, until closure of the depot in July 1931, ex-LBSCR Class D1 No.260 or No.616 were regular power. When that inveterate shed hunter Bill Camwell visited Bishops Waltham in 1936, the building had already gone, leaving just a water tank – once integral with the wooden shed – and fire cleaning point, as shown. Those engine facilities were maintained until 1958, four years before complete closure.

W.A. Camwell

Plates 27 & 28: LBSCR services to **Bognor** commenced on 1st June 1864, with a two-road shed being provided at the terminus. This served until 1902/3 and replacement by another two-road depot on a site opposite. Bognor's second shed is seen (top) when brand new, with the rear wall and sand furnace of the original shed still standing, at left. A turntable was sited by the signal box, distantly seen in the centre picture, which dates from March 1935. As may be noted the track passing the building on the left terminated on the table, as did the two shed roads. Despite electrification coming to Bognor on 2nd July 1938, the shed did not close until 1953, but remained in use for visiting engines until 1956, when it was demolished save for one wall. Even then though, turning and watering facilities were maintained until 1965.

B. Hilton collection

Plate 29: Destined to be the last new branch line shed built by the LSWR, **Bordon's** little corrugated iron depot opened with the line from Bentley, on 11th December 1905. It is seen here after about 26 years of unremarkable existence – unremarkable that is, except during the two world wars, when it serviced many of the visiting engines that traversed the branch with dense military traffic. Final closure came in 1950, by which time the building was somewhat dilapidated, but the steel framework stood until around 1957, the year in which passenger services ceased; complete closure was on 4th April 1966.

A.B. Macleod/NRM

Plates 30 & 31: **Bournemouth's** position as a pre-eminent holiday resort is entirely due to the railway, for it was but a small village when trains first ran, on 14th March 1870. The LSWR-worked Ringwood, Christchurch & Bournemouth Railway had a small shed at the terminus (named "East" after 15th June 1874), and noted in that year as being "for two engines". Anyway, the LSWR had absorbed the Ringwood company from 1st January 1874, and on 20th July 1885, extended the line to a new Bournemouth East station (renamed "Central" from 1st May 1899). A three-road turntable shed was provided at the new station and this is seen on 9th August 1902 above, from the front, and centre, from the side, with Class 348 No. 0353 employed on station pilot duties.

C.H. Eden

Plate 32: Obviously, the above shed would not have been adequate for long. So, in anticipation of opening of the Brockenhurst-Christchurch direct line, on 6th March 1888, a four-road depot was brought into use at **Bournemouth East** in the preceding year. The two buildings stood opposite each other, with a turntable and locomotive yard between, and this view distantly shows the larger building, from across the coaling and ashpit area; the year was about 1932. The turntable was sited behind the camera, being retained after the three-road shed had been removed, about 1921.

G. Coltas

Plates 33 & 34: **Bournemouth's** four-road shed is seen above, as viewed from the yard on 28th April 1928. N15 class No. 790 *Sir Villiars*, N class No. 834, X2 class No. 580 and L11 class No. 156 grace the scene, and visible between the first two is the open rear of the depot, the change from a dead-end building being made in 1921 – an improvement that doubtless was linked with the demise of the turntable shed. Below, 33 years have passed, to 20th May 1961, and a picture taken from the same point shows two main changes. The building is no longer a through-type, having been doubled in length by a rear extension, in 1936. Then, the original gabled roofs have been replaced (about 1956), by the British Railways' standard pattern of asbestos sheeting, on a steel frame.

H.C. Casserley & K. Fairey

Plate 35: A more distant picture of **Bournemouth,** taken in 1959, clearly shows the rear extension, together with the hoist provided in the late 1920s and just visible behind, the water softener added in 1938. Along with Stewarts Lane shed's BR Class 5 No. 73042, three Pacifics can be identified: Nos 34043 *Combe Martin,* 34042 *Dorchester* and 35027 *Port Line.*

G. Coltas

Plate 36: With the 9th July 1967 end of steam on the Southern Region, redundancy came to **Bournemouth** shed and its steam age paraphernalia, including this $1^1/_2$ ton capacity coaling crane No. DS60 – formerly 60S. Together with sister crane No. 61S, they were unique in being electrically driven – note the lengthy power cable looped around the buffer. Apparently No. 60S had been converted in 1923, from water tank No. LS10, at a cost of £715, and spent its entire life at Bournemouth. The picture dates from 3rd September 1967, only a short time before the engine shed and all its facilities were swept away for ever.

P. Tatlow

FOCUS ON BRICKLAYERS ARMS

Plate 37: The site of the SER's short-lived first London passenger terminus, **Bricklayers Arms'** original engine shed was a two-road structure opened in 1844. It was joined three years later by a much larger four-road building that was itself extended to eight roads about 1865. Only four years after that came another building, a six-road edifice christened "New", while the eight roader became the "Old" shed; the original two-road building was not in use by this time. That ended SER development but the SECR made one final addition to shed accommodation when the original four-road carriage shed was converted to locomotive use, being named "St Patrick's" in the process. In this well-known picture we see the Old shed in the early years of the 20th century. The 1847 section is on the right and both portions had been built with arched entrances. Note the enormous quantities of ash and the two labourers facing the Herculean task of shifting it. It serves to remind us that not all of the steam locomotive's features were attractive!

Lens of Sutton

Plate 38: This c1960 picture shows the original section of the **Bricklayers Arms** Old shed, as re-roofed by the Southern, in 1937. As may be noted, the building was of the through type and four 'bashers' are just emerging from its gloomy interior.

W.T. Stubbs collection

Plate 39: Taken on the same occasion as the preceding picture, this study reveals that the 1865 extension to the Old shed had been re-roofed in the BR style, at a date unknown. This particular building had only one of its roads – that on the right – taken through the rear wall to the turntable.

W.T. Stubbs collection

Plate 40: The **"Brick"** as it was sometimes lovingly – or otherwise – known to the men who worked there, had numerous suburban and main line passenger duties, the engines for which turns tended to gravitate to the St Patrick's shed. This is evidenced from a picture taken on 19th April 1949, when 'Schools' class Nos 30931 *King's-Wimbledon* and 30939 *Leatherhead* framed a staff 'discussion group', sublimely indifferent to the fact that they are being captured for posterity. Also on view is the knightly posterior of Stewarts Lane's No. (30)763 *Sir Bors de Ganis,* and the water softener installed as part of a late 1930's improvement scheme. It is also plain to see that this building had been re-roofed in SR times.

B. Hilton collection

Plate 41: Cudworth 'Mail' class 7ft single No. 72 poses on **Bricklayers Arms** turntable, about 1885. To put the reader in perspective, the Old shed was behind the camera, St Patrick's to the left and New – accessible only from the turntable – on the right. The wooden building behind No. 72 stands on the site of a repair shop to be built in 1934, while the turntable would be enlarged to 65ft a few years after that. The Single was built in 1865, carried the name *Excalibur* and a blue livery for a short time, was reboilered by Stirling in 1876 and withdrawn in October 1887.

NRM

Plate 42: Photographs of **Bricklayers Arms** New shed are very difficult to find! The building comprised two three-road gable-roofed sections which received severe damage at the hands of the Luftwaffe during the 'Blitz'. In later Southern and all BR times the four remaining roads in the roofless shed were used for storing engines and coal. Because of the latter it was known to some as "The Coal Hole", a gloomy name not belied by this picture, taken on a suitably depressing 11th September 1954. Ex-LBSCR Class E6 No. 32410 stands cold, wet and forlorn, and in danger of being engulfed by the straggling coal heap.

B. Morrison

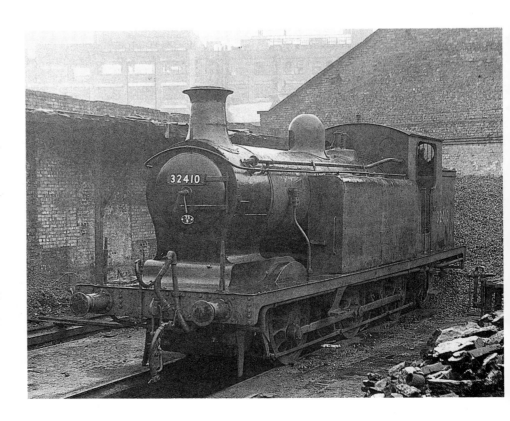

Plate 43: On that same miserable day in September 1954, Brian Morrison took refuge from the rain in **Bricklayers Arms** workshop. In the surprisingly bright interior he found Class U No. 31629 receiving large scale repairs – just about everything to do with its cylinders and valve gear was in bits! After the depot closed, on 17th June 1962, this workshop served until March 1964, becoming the only structure to survive demolition – it still stands today, in other use.

B. Morrison

Plate 44: One would have thought that as a major depot, **Bricklayers Arms** would have been provided with a breakdown crane from an early date, but this was not the case. First allocation was in October 1927, when crane No. 80S, a year old Ransomes & Rapier 36 tonner, came to the depot. It was provided with its own shelter, comprising an awning attached to the north side of the St Patrick's shed, and stayed until December 1937. The replacement for No. 80S was the brand new No. 1197S, another R&R 36 ton machine. This crane was destined to remain at the "Brick" until just before closure and it is here seen about 1959, standing beneath its canopy – in steam, as always.

P. Tatlow collection

Plate 45: Brighton's first railway was the route from Shoreham, opened on 12th May 1840; the London main line following on 21st September 1841. A locomotive allocation list dated 1st May 1844 shows 13 engines at **Brighton** – three housed in "the small shed", the rest in "the large shed" (there were also five engines in the workshop). Location and layout of the small shed have yet to be determined, but most likely it was of one-road, sited by the Shoreham line, north west of the station. Regarding the large shed, this magnificent 1860 picture shows that the 1841 building had four roads and three other entrances, which probably were not used for running purposes. Note the two turntables, coal stack and stage, and hand-powered accident crane. Occupying a cramped site north east of the station, this shed closed in 1861, to be incorporated in an expanded Brighton Works. It is sobering to think that the superb windmill in the distance, and most of the surrounding hills, have since been submerged in a sea of suburbia!

B. Matthews collection

Plate 46: Replacement for **Brighton's** first two engine sheds was this 16-road building opened in 1861, on the site of a huge chalk cliff that had taken many years to remove. Roads were numbered 1-16 from the right, with 1 and 2 originally passing through the tankhouse into the shed beyond, and out to the rear. Access from the south to Nos 1 and 2 was soon impeded by the coaling area, as may be seen in this 1900 view. The result was that the north facing two-road shed was more or less relegated to being Brighton Works' stock shed, a duty it performed until 1912, when it returned to locomotive running use – its northerly access being convenient for locomotives proceeding to main and east lines.

F. Burtt/NRM

Plate 47: Another cliché shot of **Brighton** shed from the well-known Howard Place vantage point. The year was about 1906 and is it not obvious how much more interest was created by the naming of locomotives – even lowly tank engines? Road No. 1 beneath the water tank houses a Kitson Atlantic, on a site to be occupied from around 1911 by the familiar large water softener. At that time the coaling area was moved to the bottom left hand corner of the picture, where it remained to the end, in cramped co-habitation with the turntable.

A.G. Ellis collection

Plate 48: Class H2 Atlantic No. 421 gets a lift from crane No. 16, in the yard of **Brighton** shed in 1912. Later to be named *South Foreland* the 4-4-2 clearly shows her direct lineage to Ivatt's famous examples on the GNR. No. 421 would not be withdrawn until August 1956, by which time it had covered a distance of more than 1.1 million miles. The steam crane was to be even longer lived. A 15 tonner, built in 1898 by Cowans Sheldon, No. 16 would become Southern No. 315S, move to Ashford in 1926, Ramsgate in 1946, and be renumbered DS315 by BR, before withdrawal on 9th March 1963.

F. Burtt/NRM

Plate 49: A reminder of the days of "one man – one engine", and a fairly leisurely life for both it seems. **Brighton** driver Alfred Aylwin and his C1 class (?) 0-6-0 travelled only 94,588 miles in 4 years and 2 months, which equates to an average of 1,891 miles per month, or just 70 miles a working day. Changed working conditions and hours for railwaymen, introduced after World War One, effectively put paid to the policy of single manning, and another rather special operating practice was forever lost.

F. Burtt/NRM

Plate 50: **Brighton's** tiled gabled roofs were replaced by an asbestos northlight covering in 1938. The reroofing was not total – roads 1-6 were left open to the elements and the shed's arched entrances disappeared at the same time. Yet another view from Howard Place, dating from 28th May 1950, shows the somewhat 'tatty' result, a vista which remained until closure of the shed. Not seen in the previous pictures are the hoist and wheeldrop in the yard, with a 4-4-2 in residence. These were provided around the time of World War One and must have been a considerable improvement over the methods seen in *Plate 48.*

A.G. Ellis collection

Plate 51: The long building with twin gabled roofs, seen at right in *Plate 46,* was built as a four-road carriage shed, but was marked on an 1898 plan as a wagon shop. By 1912 the Carriage & Wagon Department had moved out to Lancing and the building taken over mainly for use as **Brighton Works'** stock shed, having one road deleted, receiving a new roof of transverse pitches, and being named the "New" shed. In this interior view, dating from about 1914, we see numerous stored engines and the unusual feature of an internal crossover.

B. Hilton collection

Plate 52: After a time, **Brighton** New shed was turned over for locomotive running purposes, a practice which ended subsequent to the 1933 electrification. Later again, the building passed into yet another phase, as a workshop for the Road Motor Engineer, such use continuing until closure of the entire engine shed complex in June 1964, with subsequent demolition. This print dates from around 1934, with the still-operative New shed distantly visible across Montpelier turntable and engine sidings. The 60ft table was installed in 1910, in replacement of a 42ft version, which in the late 1880s had been moved to Montpelier from a site nearer the station.

NRM

Plate 53: Not an engine shed, but one of the fairly numerous outstations where engines and crews could rest between duties, with facilities for turning, watering and fire cleaning. This is **Bromley North,** opened on 1st January 1878 and seen here about 1910. Note the small turntable – actually 45ft – a glimpse of an ashpit, and the water tank, complete with a charmingly "potted" pumping engine chimney protruding from a shrub. This servicing point was removed when the station was rebuilt as part of an electrification scheme completed on 28th February 1926.

B. Matthews collection

Plate 54: **Bude's** potential as a place from which to ship Cornish china clay was what first attracted the LSWR. But, it was not until 10th August 1898 that the branch line to Holsworthy was extended to the North Cornish coast. A small shed was provided at the terminus, seen here in July 1933 with a visiting 4-4-0; normal allocation was one tank engine, usually an M7. Bude's popularity as a holiday resort grew and by the late 1930s, two tanks were allocated during the summer for dealing with the extra traffic, including through coaches. Dieselisation caused the shed's demise in September 1964, with complete closure of the line only two years later.

A.G. Ellis collection

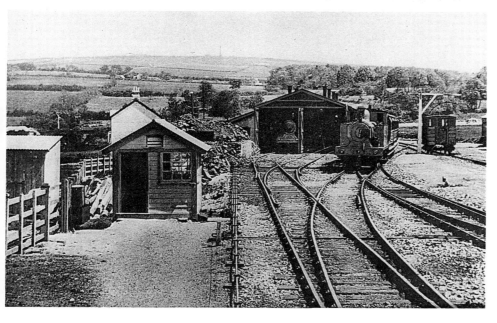

Plates 55-57: First rails to Callington were those of the 3ft 6in gauge East Cornwall Mineral Railway, which was opened in 1872 and incorporated into the Plymouth, Devonport & South Western Junction Railway 22 years later. In 1908, the PDSW altered the line to standard gauge and built a new shed at **Callington,** viewed here about 1910, with a train approaching the station. At centre, in a photograph dating from 1935, it may be seen that the shed had been 'turned around', with the entrance now facing away from the terminus; this alteration taking place in early SR days. Unknown, however, is the date of the next re-modelling, the results of which are visible in the lower picture: note that the shed building had been shortened and a new, higher pitched gable roof applied. The three prints show two of the PDSW engines which worked the branch all their lives. 757 class 0-6-2T, SR No. 758 *Lord St Levan* and No. 30757 *Earl of Mount Edgcumbe;* in SR times these engines were repaired, washed-out etc, at the main depot, Plymouth Friary. Callington's little wooden shed was Western Region 'property' in the last years leading up to closure in September 1964, when the allocation was three LMS design 2-6-2Ts.
S.C. Nash collection, B. Matthews & S.C. Nash

Plate 58: A very rare view of the five-road turntable shed at **Cannon Street,** not long after its 1st September 1866 opening. Sited at the opposite end of the Thames bridge to the station, this depot saw allocation of such SER types as Class 205 0-4-2WTs, for Charing Cross shuttles and suburban turns, with, in the late 1880s, early '90s, Class Q 0-4-4Ts, Nos 330, 344-346 and 365. Then, in December 1895, came main line power in the guise of Class F 4-4-0s Nos 60, 130, 143 and 226, these being replaced in September 1898 by Class B Nos 440, 444 and 454. The shed ceased to have a formal allocation in SECR days and was closed as part of the 1926 electrification scheme. Part of the building was incorporated into an electricity sub-station and as such, remains today.

S.C. Nash collection

Plate 59: Canterbury saw its first main line SER trains on 6th February 1846, although the company had been working the Canterbury & Whitstable Railway for two years previously. A shed was erected at **Canterbury West** and it will forever be associated with the C&W line and the Class R and R1 0-6-0Ts that worked it. One such engine – SER No. 10, came new in December 1890, and stayed long enough to work the last official service over the C&W, as BR No. 31010, on 29th November 1952. Here we see sister engine No. A126 outside the shed in 1926, a vista that within a year, would be obscured by erection of a signal bridge between the water tank and shed. The depot closed in 1955.

Lens of Sutton

Plate 60: Another old and rare print – **Caterham** station about 1865, with the rear of the engine shed visible at left. This is the only picture so far found of the depot, which opened with the Caterham Railway on 5th August 1856, and was closed in 1877, to be converted to a goods shed. It seems there was a replacement shed, because locomotives continued to be allocated to Caterham – SER Class 235 0-4-4WTs Nos 235, 237 and 239, in 1884-5 for example – but it is shrouded in obscurity and no photograph has yet been seen. Closure of this second 'facility' came in 1898, with the opening of Purley shed.

J. Spence collection

Plate 61: The LSWR branch to Chard (Town) opened on 8th May 1863, with 2-2-2WTs Nos 13 *Orion* and 76 *Firefly* working services, until both were withdrawn in 1872. They were housed in a single road shed at the terminus, which was by-passed on 11th September 1866 by the line to Chard (Joint), where the LSWR shared a turntable at the Bristol & Exeter Railway engine shed (GWR from 1876). When **Chard Town** depot closed is not known. An Ordnance Survey map of the 1890s shows the building still in existence, and a locomotive allocation list of March 1900 had Class O2 No. 117 based at Chard, but she could have been at the GWR depot. Whatever, the building had long been gone by the time Bill Camwell visited the site on 13th April 1936. He found only the office and remains of the coal stage as shown here; the shed stood between these edifices and the camera.

W.A. Camwell

Plate 62: Chertsey was reached by the LSWR's branch from Weybridge on St Valentine's Day, 1848, and remained a terminal station until the line was extended to Virginia Water, on 1st October 1866. A two-road locomotive shed was provided at **Chertsey,** probably from the outset, being operational for two engines usually, until electrification of the line in January 1937. This c1931 view suggests a more modern building than one dating from 1848. However, plans reveal that it had the archaic feature of exterior buttresses to the side walls, so, perhaps it also once had similarly vintage arched entrances, the removal of which entailed provision of new end walls and roof?

A.B. Macleod/NRM

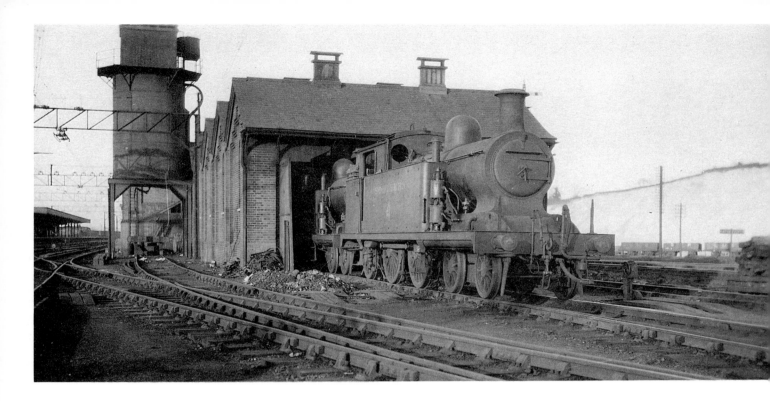

Plates 63 & 64: The **LBSCR** opened a new terminus and engine shed at **Coulsdon North** – known at first as "Stoats Nest" – at the relatively late date of 1900. The two-road shed housed engines working outer suburban passenger and goods trains, and it is seen here, above, in 1927 and below, from the rear about 1912. The top picture shows evidence of the LBSCR 6,600V ac overhead electrification works, which commenced operation, at the London end, on 1st December 1909. However, it was some years before the catenary reached Coulsdon, which explains why it is absent from the lower view and, consequently, why more engines were present, being parked 'up the yard', by the coal stage, due to lack of space. Nevertheless, it was the new form of motive power which finally wrote finis to Coulsdon shed, with passenger workings ceasing in 1928, and goods in June 1929. Demolition followed, except for the rear wall and offices, which did not finally succumb until the entire station area was cleared in 1985/6.

S.C. Nash collection & Author's collection

Plate 65: The first locomotive shed on the Isle of Wight was that of the Cowes & Newport Railway, opened at **Cowes** on 16th June 1862. That one-road wooden depot and adjoining carriage shed are depicted in 1876, showing storm damage received on 29th September that year. Eleven years later, the C&NR was incorporated into the Isle of Wight Central Railway and in 1892 the new owners rebuilt Cowes station, such work necessitating closure and removal of the engine shed.

T. Cooper collection

Plate 66: This 1937 picture shows the second SER shed at **Deal,** opened mid-June 1881. It replaced a two-road building provided on the same site when the SER first reached there on 1st July 1847. Early allocations of the three-road depot were quite small – for instance, Class 73 0-4-2WTs Nos 14 and 41, for some years, up to their withdrawal in June 1893. Then, on 15th October 1898, it is known only three engines were stationed, although rosters were increased during SECR times. Closure came in September 1930, but the turntable was retained and the shed turned over to other uses. In fact, it was regarded as sufficiently indispensable to have a new roof provided late in SR days, during which the separate entrances were removed. The building was finally done away with in the early 1960s.

S.C. Nash collection

Plates 67 & 68: Faded copy negatives of photographs dating from 1911, depict what could be termed as London's first engine shed – **Deptford,** on the London & Greenwich Railway. Opened from Bermondsey to Deptford on 8th February 1836, and extended on to Greenwich 14th December in the same year, the L&GR built a single-road shed at Deptford, seen here in the top picture, with a signal box spanning the entrance. The wooden coaling platform is in the foreground and that hemispherical structure appears to have been the depot's water tank. Deptford shed closed when the SER leased the L&GR from 1st January 1845, but due to congestion at Bricklayers Arms, was reopened in 1864. At that time the former L&GR works was also used for locomotive running purposes and the lower view, taken from the signal box, shows the site of that three-road building (demolished 1909), under and beyond the stacked sleepers. Final closure came in 1903, as a 'knock-on' effect of the opening of new sheds at Slades Green and Orpington.

S.C. Nash collection

Plate 69: LSWR trains first entered Plymouth on 17th May 1876, initially running via the GWR's Launceston branch from Lydford. The LSWR's terminus was at **Devonport,** which included this two-road shed, seen in 1964; the photographer was standing with the site of the turntable immediately behind. The PDSWR line arrived from the north on 2nd June 1890, with Devonport station becoming "through". The shed continued to provide shunters for Devonport Goods and Stonehouse Pool, even after a new locomotive depot opened at Plymouth Friary Station, on 1st July 1891. However, when the second Friary shed was brought into service in 1908, Devonport closed, to see further uses – a furniture removals store and bottling plant among them.

S.C. Nash

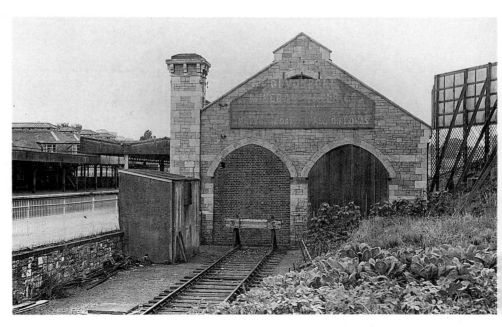

Plates 70 & 71: Southampton & Dorchester Railway services commenced on 1st June 1847, with a two-road shed provided in Dorset's county town. Traffic growth caused the LSWR to expand **Dorchester** shed to four-roads in 1875. Both sections of the depot are visible in these prints, that above dating from 4th October 1931, that below, from 18th May 1952. The first building, on the left, was made in brick, while the 1875 extension was constructed in timber, above dwarf brick walls. It may be noted that between 1931 and 1952, the second section's wooden gable (and roof probably) had given way to asbestos, while the central smoke vent of the 1847 building had also been replaced. Notice too how every locomotive – even tank types – faces east.

A.W.Croughton, courtesy J. Lucking & T.J. Edgington

Plate 72: **Dorchester's** importance declined in latter SR and early BR times, but 14 engines were still stationed in August 1950. However, with reduction to sub-shed status in 1955, the number of outstationed locomotives dwindled to five, and by 18th February 1957, when this photograph was taken, closure was only five months away. In anticipation, the shed's wooden section had already succumbed, revealing the shearlegs to the atmosphere for the first time in 82 years. After closure, the depot site was cleared and later used for housing.

J. Lucking

Plate 73: In another view of **Dorchester** dating from 18th February 1957, visiting ex-GWR 2-6-0 No. 6384 is about to proceed to the turntable. Weymouth ex-GWR shed's table was undergoing repair at that time, meaning all locomotives had to travel to Dorchester for turning. The 50ft diameter of the turntable there effectively excluded the 'Hall' class normally used on the Western Region's services to Weymouth, so all such traffic was temporarily placed in the competent care of Moguls. Perhaps in gratitude for photographing themselves and their engine, the crew of No. 6384 gave the photographer a footplate ride back to his home town of Weymouth – as he says – happy days!

J. Lucking

Plate 74: An inadequate, but nonetheless priceless print, in that it shows the photographically shy LBSCR shed at **Dorking** – dimly visible behind the signal post. This building had opened with the line from Leatherhead, on 4th March 1867, and two months later was providing motive power for the route to Horsham. Typically, allocations were very static – for example:

1896: Class D1 Nos 229/38/89/90/1 (5).

1911: Class D1 Nos 229/60/88/91, 358, 633 (6).

1921: Class D1 Nos 229/44/83/8/91 (5).

Appropriately, long-term resident No. 229 originally carried the name *Dorking,* while equally persistent No. 291 was *Deepdene.*

The late E. Wallis collection, by permission of D. Wallis & Mrs M. Mason

Plate 75: In 1922, **Dorking's** wooden shed proved the loser in a struggle with gale force winds, and what little remained after the storm passed was immediately removed. However, for a few more years the depot had to continue functioning, which it did, in an al fresco manner. This picture dates from 24th May 1926 and shows a 'full house' of six Class D1s or D3s standing on the old shed roads, and a solitary Class I2 4-4-2T; numbers visible are, left to right, B216, B382 and B17. Note the wooden hut provided for enginemen, and that coaling was effected from a stack. These basic amenities were destined to disappear three years later, as a result of an electrification scheme completed on 3rd March 1929.

H.C. Casserley

Plate 76: A panoramic view of **Dover Priory**, thought to date from the late 1880s, from the hill through which the LCDR main line tunnelled, just out of picture, to the right. The station opened on 22nd July 1861, complete with goods and carriage sheds, and a four-road engine shed, seen right of the station, with longitudinal smoke vents along the roof ridges. Also on view are the depot's turntable, water tank and line of wagons leading to the coaling area adjacent to the tunnel mouth; a few years later a larger turntable would be installed on the coaling site. Priory remained the principal Dover shed after formation of the SECR and was finally closed in 1932, being superseded by an **SR**-built shed erected four years earlier at Dover Marine.

Author's collection

Plates 77 & 78: **Dover's** first engine shed was that of the SER, at Dover Town, which came into use on 7th February 1844 and comprised two single road buildings, sited one each side of the line at the opposite (western) end of Archcliffe Tunnel to the station. Before long – the date is not known – another engine shed, of four roads, was erected beside Town station, at which time the single-road depot south of the line went out of use. However, the other single-road building remained as some sort of annexe to the main shed and that survivor is distantly visible above, in the background of this 20th September 1910 picture of 0-6-0 No. 90 and train. Notice that the cliff through which the short Archcliffe Tunnel passed had been removed. Below, from a date around 1905, comes this shot of the four-road depot, with a selection of SECR 4-4-0s in residence. It seems likely that both buildings finally closed with the station, in 1914, but despite their fairly late existence, these two photographs are the only ones that have so far been found.

K. Nunn collection/LCGB & Lens of Sutton

Plate 79: Southern Railway concrete at **Dover Marine.** This five-road shed opened in 1928 and is depicted here about ten years later, in a view from the coal stage – also made in concrete. The SR did not provide a mechanical coaler, probably because of earlier experience with coal pulverisation and/or the fact that the depot was built on reclaimed land, which might not have given sufficiently firm foundations. Otherwise, the shed was efficiently planned, with a spacious yard, 65ft turntable, water treatment plant and well equipped workshop. During World War Two Dover shed was right in the front line, dealing first with much of the heavy Dunkirk evacuation traffic, and subsequently being closed for a time due to German shelling of the port. The depot survived all that, but could not face up to the tide of electrification, which brought about closure in 1961.

Author's collection

Plate 80: An ex-LBSCR engine, at a Southern-built shed in ex-LCDR/SER territory, in **BR** days! Class D1 No. 2359 (formerly LBSCR, No. 359 *Egmont*) performs stationary boiler duties outside the repair shop at **Dover**, on 14th July 1950. Thirteen months later, No. 2359 would be replaced in this task by E5 Class 0-6-2T No. 32593, which itself was withdrawn in January 1956. It is not known which engine(s) continued the job of "kettle" in the shed's remaining five years.

H.C. Casserley

Plate 81: A delightful platform-end piece at **Eastbourne** from around 1906, with 'Gladstone' class No. 215 *Salisbury* and train running in past the 1876 part-roundhouse. What appear to be three Edwardian train spotters (somewhat inappropriately attired!) are having something explained while perhaps, the departing railwayman was going across to the depot, to find out for them what was "on shed"?

Author's collection

Plate 82: This portrait of **Eastbourne's** eight-stall roundhouse comes from the mid-1890s, and shows "Terrier" No. 65 *Tooting* about to set 'foot' on the 45ft turntable. The depot was the second to be built in the town. The first, a two-road straight shed, dated from opening of the railway, on 14th May 1849. That shed apparently survived a move of the station in 1866 and provision of a new station in 1871, before succumbing to the round shed five years later. (Incidentally, the 1871 station was itself replaced after only 15 years – things certainly never were static at Eastbourne!)

B. Matthews collection

Plate 83: A marvellous vista of **Eastbourne** locomotive yard in 1912, reputedly on the date of closure of the part-roundhouse. The two Sunday-best dressed men were almost certainly the shed foremen, proudly posing with their charges in a valedictory picture.

F. Burtt/NRM

Plate 84: Each year, the **LBSCR** used to run staff special trains from London, for the Stationmaster's and Inspector's Mutual Aid Fund. **Eastbourne** was often the destination, the shed hosting the locomotives off the specials, for which much embellishment was the order of the day! This may be appreciated from a photograph dating from c1900, showing the highly decorated front ends of the two engines selected to haul that year's specials – one each from Victoria and London Bridge. Unfortunately the identities of the locomotives are not known.

F. Burtt/NRM

Plates 85 & 86: Cramped accommodation was the hallmark of **LBSCR** engine sheds and Eastbourne's roundhouse was no exception! So, in the first decade of the 20th century the railway decided to build a new locomotive depot. What materialised in 1911/12 was, without question, the best laid out of all LBSCR sheds, with ample room for men and machines. The only possible disadvantage lay in its distance from the station, which probably explains why the roundhouse's turntable was retained after demolition of that building, to serve until electrification in 1935. **Eastbourne's** seven-road shed is seen above when brand-new, and below, in 1948. By the latter date its importance had dwindled, despite the number of engines to be seen – many of them were in store. The depot continued to function though, albeit in semi-derelict condition, until the end of steam, finally being removed at the close of the 1960s.

F. Burtt/NRM & S.C. Nash

FOCUS ON EASTLEIGH

Plates 87 & 88: The next four photographs magnificently portray the large (270ft wide by 345ft long), 15-road shed at **Eastleigh,** in 1910. The depot opened in 1903, in replacement of another large shed at nearby Northam and, even closer, a brace of two-road sheds at Eastleigh (Bishopstoke) station – although they had not appeared on any engine allocation list since at least 1898. The picture above shows the north end of Eastleigh shed. Notice the repair shop on the right and the huge water tank at left – its supporting tankhouse contained an enginemens' dormitory, which could not have meant much restful sleep was to be had, especially on the top floor! Below, is the south end of the shed complete with neat coal stack and a strangely deserted look. Presumably the shed staff had "cleared the decks" for the LSWR's official photographer!

NRM

Plates 89 & 90: The good design of the LSWR's steel and glass roofs is apparent from these light and airy interior shots of **Eastleigh.**
At top we see the various notice boards, signing on book, workshop doors and enginemens' lobby. Somewhere around here was the
foreman's office, a place to be avoided by any visitor who did not have a permit! (In the author's opinion, numbers obtained by the
strictly illegal practice of "bunking" a shed were that bit more valuable. Incidentally, on a personal "Bunking Difficulty" scale of
1-10, Eastleigh rated 5.) The lower print depicts the depot's lifting shop with not one, but two shearlegs and a good complement of
line shaft-powered machine tools – very necessary with an allocation of over 100 locomotives to care for.

NRM

Plates 91 & 92: Typical yard scenes at **Eastleigh,** where much variety and interest was provided by the constant procession of engines passing to and from the Works. The debt owned by railway enthusiasts to Mr H.C. Casserley for his prolific photography can well be appreciated from these two pictures. They were taken in the last year of both the LSWR and SR (actual dates being 15th April 1922 and 20th May 1947 respectively), events separated by a quarter of a century, from a career spanning more than four decades. Above, three of Eastleigh's roof gables form a backdrop to an Adams Radial tank, three assorted Southampton Docks shunters and at right Class T14 "Paddlebox" No. 462. In the bottom picture is evidence of the short-lived oil burning period, conceived by a panicky government and overall, an expensive non-event. Class T9 Nos 113 and 280 are fresh out of shops following conversion to oil firing. Both were not returned to coal burning, however, being stored by Autumn 1948 and withdrawn in May 1951.

H.C. Casserley

Plate 93: Another southern aspect of **Eastleigh,** dating from 14th September 1950, showing how, during its first two years, BR had re-roofed the shed. See also the depleted coal stack and new boiler house on the left of the depot, installed for fuel pumping purposes in the abortive oil-burning scheme.

B. Hilton

Plate 94: Despite its size and importance, **Eastleigh** never was provided with a mechanical coaling plant, fuelling being effected from a long double-sided ramp coaler, equipped with six tips. This can partly be seen in *Plate 87,* when it was patently of wooden construction. However, it is a brick structure that provides the background to two of the last types of steam engine to be seen at the shed. When the stage had been rebuilt is not known, but by the time this picture was taken, on 9th May 1964, its work was being supplemented by use of a steam crane, a situation that pertained throughout the shed's closing days. The end came in fact, on 9th July 1967, after which demolition preceded re-use of part of the site for a diesel depot.

K. Fairey

Plate 95: **Eastleigh's** first steam breakdown crane was LSWR No. 3, a Dunlop & Bell 15 ton machine, ex-Nine Elms. That was followed by No. 1, a Stothert & Pitt 20 tonner, which in time, gave way to the crane portrayed here, along with its two match wagons, on 1st June 1962. This 36 ton capacity Ransomes & Rapier device had been delivered to the LSWR in 1918, becoming No. 5. Stationed initially at Nine Elms, it received number 35S under SR ownership and was moved to Fratton in 1937, before coming to Eastleigh in June 1946. Designated No. DS35 by BR, the crane was withdrawn on 9th January 1965. Its replacement was Ransomes & Rapier 45 tonner, No. DS1560, itself superseded in April 1965 by Cowans Sheldon 75 ton diesel-hydraulic crane No. DB965185. That monster saw out Eastleigh shed's final days.

P. Tatlow collection

Plate 96: A GWR/LSWR Joint concern, the Easton & Church Hope Railway ran from Portland to Easton, on the Portland peninsula; it was completed in 1900. An E&CHR engine shed was built for the line's opening, but survived only four years, when its place was taken by this LSWR-built depot, seen here in 1911. It was in August of that year that Dorchester shed's allocation of Class O2 0-4-4Ts comprised Nos 202, 214, 233 and 234, and one of those would normally have been at **Easton**, outstationed from the LSWR sub-shed at Weymouth (after 1938, from the GWR's Weymouth depot). Easton's passenger services ran until 1952, at which point the little stone shed closed, soon to be demolished.

H. Garratt collection

Plates 97 & 98: First ideas for motive power on the West Croydon-Epsom (Town) line were for the atmospheric type, but the poor showing of that system elsewhere, caused the LBSCR to adhere to conventional locomotive haulage. Accordingly, a two-road engine shed was installed at the **Epsom** terminus, some years after the line's 10th May 1847 opening, but before its extension to Leatherhead, on 8th August 1859. It is seen in the top picture on 24th May 1926, with typical suburban tank engine residents. Below is an interior view giving a clear impression of the rear office, work bench and boiler; note too the sleeper-laid floor. The Class D1 0-4-2T No. 607 was formerly No. 7 *Bermondsey;* it received its new number in July 1907 and was withdrawn in December 1912. The picture therefore dates from that five year, five month period. Epsom shed closed on 3rd March 1929, following completion of an electrification scheme.

H.C. Casserley & Lens of Sutton

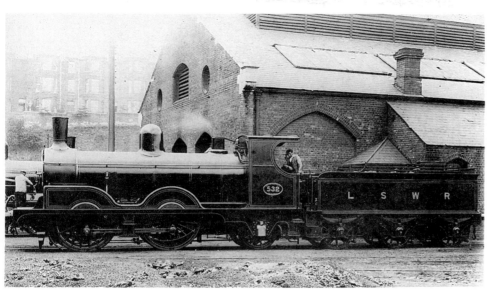

Plates 99 & 100: Two rare glimpses of the substantial, but very elusive LSWR shed at **Exeter Queen Street** (later "Central"). Opened by the Exeter & Yeovil Railway on 19th July 1860, the depot closed again in 1887, when the first Exmouth Junction shed came into service. However, Queen Street's three-road building remained in use for servicing engines until mostly demolished in the early 1900s, but even then, the turntable and coal stage were retained until 1930. At top is the only known picture of a sizeable piece of Queen Street shed, with 'Jubilee' class 0-4-2 No. 532 parked in front. (The reader can get a better overall idea of how the building looked by turning to *Plates 315-317,* showing Yeovil shed. That was also of E&YR origins and virtually identical to Queen Street.) Below, in a c1912 view from a road overbridge, with the station behind us, we can pinpoint Queen Street shed's position. The carriages at extreme right are stabled on the former shed roads; behind them, still standing, is the depot's former south wall – compare the pointed arch alcoves. *S.C. Nash collection & H. Garratt collection*

Plate 101: Services over the Exeter & Exmouth Railway were worked by the LSWR from opening, on 1st May 1861, based on a single-road wooden shed at **Exmouth**; the E&ER was absorbed in 1866. On 1st June 1903, Exmouth depot commenced working the new line to Sidmouth Junction, a route which ran via Budleigh Salterton, where a one-road shed closed in consequence. By the mid-1920s Exmouth's building was life-expired, so in 1927/8 a replacement was put up on approximately the same site. That concrete-built shed is seen here about 1930, showing some of the Class M7s that normally worked from there. The 0-4-4Ts would give way to LMS designed Ivatt 2-6-2Ts, before dieselisation brought about closure of the depot in 1963.

B. Matthews collection

Plate 102: Cramped conditions at Exeter Queen Street led the LSWR to seek a new site for expansion of engine shed facilities. This was found at **Exmouth Junction**, where an eleven-road depot was erected in 1887. Second of the LSWR's then new design of steel and glass gabled buildings, Exmouth Junction seems to have suffered far more severely than any of its contemporaries from the depredations of soot and damp. Graphic evidence of this comes from a photograph taken on 18th July 1925, which shows just how serious conditions were. Replacement was underway at the time, on a site immediately behind this building, but was not completed until 1929, when the depot illustrated below came into use.

H.C. Casserley

Plate 103: **Exmouth Junction's** twelve-road, northlight roofed, mainly concrete-built depot, not long after opening; a thirteenth road enters the high-roofed repair shop at left. Note the distinctive smoke vents and numbering of shed roads. The latter was a favourite Southern Railway device – something continued from LBSCR practice – which, though sensible, saw little use elsewhere, except by the North British Railway.

B. Hilton collection

Plate 104: A close-up of **Exmouth Junction's** *200 ton capacity mechanical coaler, erected under contract by the specialist firm of Mitchell Conveyor & Transporter Co. Ltd. This was the third such device on the Southern, following those initiated by the LSWR at Nine Elms and Feltham. The facility would prove a life-long problem for Exmouth Junction crews, because of breakage of the Welsh coal supplied to the depot.*

Author's collection

Plate 105: This view of **Exmouth Junction**, from the coaling tower, contains a wealth of detail. The ashpits, water cranes with attendant lighting standards, and the serried ranks of smoke vents, seemingly anchored in the 'waves' of the northlight roof. The date was around 1932 and notice how, as mentioned in the preceding caption, the mechanical coaler has 'powdered' the coal in the locomotives' bunkers.

G. Coltas

Plate 106: A latter day scene at **Exmouth Junction**, dating from early 1962, shows little change, except for removal of shed road numbers, addition of an incredibly high water tank, and the presence of Bulleid and BR Standard locomotives. However, change would come soon! The depot became a Western Region responsibility from 1963 and thus came the diesels. They outlasted steam at the shed by a year, finally leaving on closure in 1966; the building lingered until demolition in 1970. The site is today covered by a supermarket and car parks.

T.W. Nicholls

Plates 107 & 108: **Faversham's** first engine shed was a two-road affair, built by the East Kent Railway and sited immediately west of the station, opening on 25th January 1858. The EKR became the LCDR on 1st August 1859 and in the next year added another two-road shed, this time some hundreds of yards east of the station, in the fork of the lines to Canterbury and Whitstable. The second building was enlarged about 1900 by addition of a further two-road section on the north side. It seems the 1858 shed went out of use before this alteration, but the actual date is not known – even so, the building was still in existence in 1907 at least. These prints show the four-road depot at dates separated by 33 years. Above, on 13th March 1926, both sections are virtually as built, with the 1860 section at right; the structure beyond the footbridge was a wagon shop. In the lower view it is evident both sections had been re-roofed – the 1860 portion in the mid-1930s and the 1900 part some eight or nine years before this 15th May 1959 picture was taken. A further BR addition was the overhead coaling gantry spanning the shed entrance. It replaced a coal stage sited at left of the picture – the BR Standard Class 4 4-6-0 stands on the former coaling road, left. The depot closed to steam in June 1959, but diesels used it thereafter, seeing demolition of the 1860 section before they too moved away. Today the 1900 building still stands, having attained a 'listed' status thanks to the efforts of the Faversham Society.

H.C. Casserley & S.C. Nash

Plate 109: After a gestation period lengthened by World War One, **Feltham** shed opened in stages, 1922-23, thus becoming the last locomotive depot built by the LSWR. It also had the distinction of being the first major shed in Britain to be constructed in concrete (only Okehampton preceded it), thereby setting a pattern which the SR would considerably enlarge upon over the succeeding decade and a half. This picture dates from the late 1920s and shows the southern end of the six-road 'through' building.

B. Hilton collection

Plate 110: **Feltham's** 200 ton coaler is depicted here soon after its completion in 1923. Another product of the Mitchell Conveyor & Transporter Co. Ltd, it differs in a number of respects from the same company's later structure at Exmouth Junction *(Plate 104)*. The SR would also make changes, as may be noted in the previous plate, in that the wagon hoist and tipping area were enclosed in corrugated cladding, in an attempt to keep down flying dust – a major problem with such mechanised coaling plants everywhere.

Author's collection

Plate 111: The north end of an empty-looking **Feltham** on 25th September 1963, showing how the northlight roof's glazing and smoke vents had suffered somewhat, over the years. Note the repair shop at left. This depot survived until the end of steam on the Southern Region, closing on 9th July 1967 and being superseded by a diesel depot built to serve the large marshalling yard. Nowadays, even that diesel shed and yard are but memories.

W.T. Stubbs collection

Plate 112: **Feltham** was renowned for its allocation of large goods tank engines. This scene, from 25th February 1963, was late in those locomotives' days, as evidenced by their stored condition. The three Class H16 4-6-2Ts (with No. 30518 still sporting the pre-1956 BR emblem), and Class W 2-6-4T (right) evoke undying memories in the author's mind. His favourite spotting locations beside Neasden or Cricklewood sheds were always enlivened by the sight of H16s, Ws and especially Feltham's other 'big boys', the Class G16 4-8-0Ts, on goods work over the North & South Western Junction line. In fact, all bar a handful of Feltham's 60-plus allocation of all types had been 'copped' before the shed was first visited!

T. Wright

Plate 113: A Stirling Class F 4-4-0 speeds an 'up' SER express past **Folkestone Junction** sheds in about 1898. The use of the plural is correct, because there are in fact two sheds visible – a pair of small single-road buildings standing back to back, with that facing Martello Tunnel mostly shrouded in smoke. It is not known if both had been provided for opening of the line, on 18th December 1843, but probably they were so, to house the initial allocation of three Bury 0-4-0s, Nos 107, 108 and 111. They were superseded in July 1851 by three 'Bulldog' class Intermediate Shaft 0-4-0Ts, which in turn gave way, in March 1877, to three Mansell 0-6-0Ts, Nos 152-154. They handed over to a trio of Class R 0-6-0Ts, bearing the same numbers, in 1892, eight years before the two little sheds were replaced by a new depot.

S.C. Nash collection

Plate 114: **Folkestone Junction's** 1900 shed, as seen in November 1958, with the famous Rs – by then re-classified R1 – still holding sway. Five are (just) visible in this picture, (plus a PW "roller skate" Wickham trolley), out of the allocation of six, sub-shedded from 74C, Dover. But, after 66 years, these 0-6-0Ts days were numbered as, in the month preceding this photograph, ex-GWR 0-6-0PT No. 9770 had been on trial on the shed's duties, which mainly concerned working the notorious Harbour Incline.

T. Wright

Plate 115: That the pannier tank's trial had proved successful is evidenced by this view of **Folkestone Junction**, taken on 26th March 1959, 24 days after Nos 4601/10/6/26/30/1 arrived to replace the R1s. But, as may be expected, the Western Region did not send anything from its First Division and these panniers were best described as "a rough lot"! However, Ashford Works – *not* Swindon – got to grips with the problem, after which the foreigners were considered very good indeed. They were joined at Folkestone in March 1960 by Class E6 0-6-2Ts Nos 32410 and 32415, for ballasting and permanent way duties, in connection with electrification work, completion of which brought about closure of the shed in 1961.

Dr T.A. Gough

Plate 116: There was another shed at **Folkestone**, the little-known and rarely photographed single-road building beside the Harbour station. Opening seems to have been in 1881, when SER No. 313, a Manning Wardle G class 0-4-0ST, arrived to work the port area. Plans show that around 1910 the original 'through' engine shed was replaced by a slightly larger dead-end building on a site some 130ft to the west. What occasioned this alteration is not known, but the new shed seems to have served only until No. 313 moved away in 1919. After that the building saw many more years' alternative use – including as a bullion store apparently. It is visible here around the late 1950s, with the remains of a steam crane parked outside – doubtless either the Cowans Sheldon, or Smith's of Rodley machines ordered for harbour duties at the same time as No. 313.

D.W. Winkworth

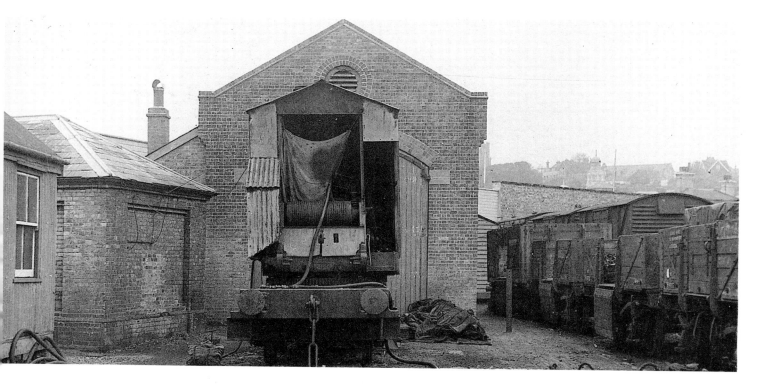

Plates 117 & 118: Portsmouth was reached by the LBSCR on 14th June 1847, and by the LSWR on 1st October 1848. The two companies shared a four-road shed near Town station (the Harbour station opened on 2nd October 1876), until 1891, when a replacement came into use. That too was a joint depot, a square 'roundhouse' – the only one of its genre to be employed by any of the Southern's constituents. Sited at **Fratton**, the shed had separate coaling facilities for each company, with both also having roundhouse stalls strictly allocated, but accessed via a mutually used turntable of course! The picture above shows the LBSCR's coal platform, with the shed behind, in about 1905; an LSWR locomotive is just visible beyond the right-hand 'Gladstone' 0-4-2. In the lower print, from c1900, both coal stages are seen, with only a solitary LSWR Adams Radial tank, and interested footplatemen, on view. It may also be discerned that there was standing room at the roundhouse's rear.

B. Matthews collection & F. Burtt/NRM

Plate 119: A view of that rear area at **Fratton**, showing how the shed had been re-roofed following wartime damage. The most valuable feature of the picture is that it shows one of the elusive oil-fired engines in steam, and actually in the process of being fuelled. The building immediately right of T9 class No. 713 was the boiler/pump house put up specially for the oil-burning project, and an example of how much money was wasted in that short-lived enterprise. The date was 11th September 1948 and in the next month No. 713 would be placed in store, to languish until withdrawn, in April 1951.

H.C. Casserley

Plate 120: Sunlight fitfully pierces **Fratton's** gloomy interior to illuminate "Terrier" No. 32640, on 21st June 1956. At that time, and until closure on 2nd November 1959, the depot's shed code was 70F, but the engine carries a 75A plate – Brighton, very appropriately, for that was its name in LBSCR days. At one time it became Isle of Wight Central Railway No. 11 in 1902, then No. W11 *Newport*, returning to the mainland in 1947. Incidentally, after closure, Fratton depot saw visiting engines until 1967, not being demolished until two years after that.

K. Fairey

Plate 121: The misty, but only known photograph of the **Freshwater** depot of the Freshwater, Yarmouth & Newport Railway on the Isle of Wight. The FY&NR opened on 10th September 1888, with a shed provided at Freshwater for the IWCR engines that ran all services. That shed was destroyed in an unknown way in 1890, being replaced in the same year. Then, in 1908, another building was authorised, sited beside the 1890 shed as seen in this 1920 picture; which shed dated from when is not clear. The IWCR worked the FY&NR until 30th June 1913, from when the latter took over, utilising two engines and a petrol railcar. Closure came when the FY&NR was belatedly grouped into the SR, on 1st August 1923.

S.C. Nash collection

Plate 122: Known as "New Brompton" for some years after its 1885 opening, we here see the LCDR shed at **Gillingham** (Kent), with its decorative brickwork and arched entrances. This depot had the distinction of sharing duties with two others – Strood, in SECR times, up to the early SR era, and Faversham thereafter. The picture dates from 17th May 1959, one year and one month before closure, and subsequent demolition.

S.C. Nash

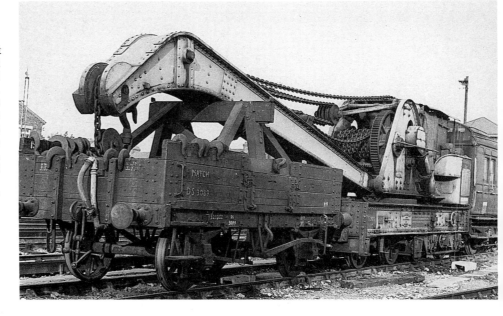

Plate 123: **Gillingham** received its first and only steam breakdown crane about 1934. This is seen here, stabled as usual in the goods yard, probably about 1958. No. DS202 was a 15 ton Cowans Sheldon product of 1899, delivered to the SER as its No. L3, stationed at Ashford. Moved to Stewarts Lane at a date unknown, it became SR No. 202S, before serving at Gillingham until withdrawn on 3rd November 1962.

P. Tatlow

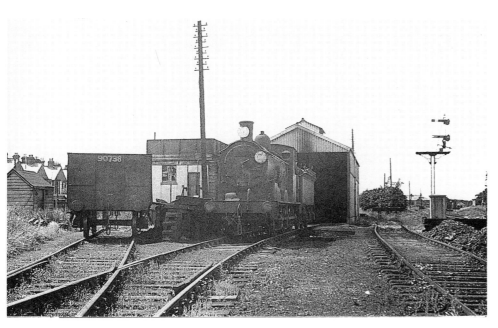

Plates 124 & 125: The line from Bishopstoke to Gosport was completed on 29th November 1841, but did not open until 7th February 1842, due to the initially unsafe condition of Fareham Tunnel. A two-road shed was put up at **Gosport** for the opening and it is seen at top when about 90 years old, with 'Jubilee' class No. 644 passing, on its way to the station. In its 99th, or possibly 100th year, the shed was heavily damaged in the 'Blitz', but a single-road corrugated asbestos replacement was quickly put up on the same site, this being seen (centre) around 1949. The first shed's coal platform and water tank had survived the air raid and continued to serve until the depot closed, with cessation of passenger services, on 8th June 1953; complete closure of the branch came in January 1969.

B. Matthews collection & H. Garratt collection

Plate 126: Absorbing the Gravesend Railway in 1883, the LCDR completed the line on 10th May 1886. A 50ft turntable was installed at Gravesend West Street and a two-road, two-engine, shed 1/2 mile out, near Rosherville station, which served the (at that time) famous Rosherville Gardens. The reason behind this was that Rosherville was in a different local authority area and attracted cheaper rates! One engine, 'Acis' class 0-6-0 No. 119 (formerly *Amphitrite*), was allocated in December 1895, and it seems a minimal allocation pertained until closure, around Grouping; in latter times apparently the depot was known as "West Street". The only illustration found of the obscure **Gravesend Rosherville** depot is this one, showing a portion of the building beyond the overbridge.

S.C. Nash collection

FOCUS ON GUILDFORD

Plate 127: LSWR metals were extended from Woking to Guildford on 5th May 1845 and a two-road engine shed built at the terminus. Lines advanced from Guildford to Farnham and Godalming, on 4th and 15th October 1849 respectively, Havant on 24th January 1859, and Surbiton on 2nd February 1885. By that time **Guildford** station and shed were no longer large enough to cope with all those services, so they were swept away in a rebuilding scheme which was completed in 1887. Both buildings are seen in this unique picture, which dates from the late 1860s; the locomotive depot may be seen at left, with three smoke vents on the roof.

Lens of Sutton

Plate 128: The 1887 replacement depot at **Guildford** was this half-roundhouse, itself extended about ten years after opening, by adding a seven-road straight shed at the rear of the section closest to the tunnel – its roof is just visible in this print, which dates from circa 1930. It is worth noting that this depot and its predecessor housed LBSCR engines after nearby Bramley shed blew down in an 1882 gale. For example, "Terriers" Nos 36 *Bramley* and 77 *Wonersh* at first, and Class C 0-6-0 No. 420 from the 1890s. All carried Guil[d] code, but returned to Horsham at weekends, for maintenance. Such outstationing ceased with the Grouping of course.

Author's collection

Plates 129 & 130: These plates show, above, **Guildford** being re-roofed by **BR** in about 1953, and below, the results, seen some seven years later. Notice in the upper photograph, the straight shed section and how the grounded coach body near the 55ft turntable, which served as a stores, was by 1960 superseded by a custom-built concrete edifice. See also the breakdown train with, in both these prints, is crane No. DS1561, a 45 ton Ransomes & Rapier machine that had come to Guildford, brand new, in August 1940. Its predecessor, since Edwardian times, had been an 1880 Jessop & Appleby 10 tonner, LSWR No. 2, SR No. 31S. Guildford's crane was downgraded somewhat, when in June 1962, No. DS1561 moved to Ashford, being replaced by No. DS80 (SR No. 80S), a 1926 Ransomes & Rapier 36 ton device that saw out the shed's remaining days, to July 1967, whence it became 'Regional Spare'.

P. Tatlow & B. Matthews collection

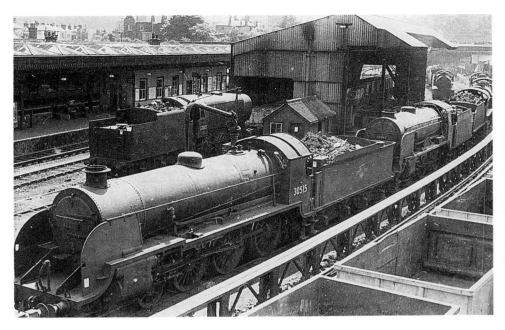

Plate 131: **Guildford** roundhouse's coaling plant was some distance from the depot, beside the station. In fact, it stood on almost the exact site of the town's first shed and is seen here with a typical Sunday morning line-up, sometime in 1957.

N. Hamshere

Plate 132: **Guildford** was known for its diminutive shed pilot engines, which used to manoeuvre dead locomotives about the depot. It is interesting to note the (known) variety of locomotives used on this duty:

    1892 - 6/1897: Manning Wardle 0-4-0ST No. 407 *Pioneer* (and 10/1915 - 2/1919).
    6/1897 - 1909/10: Beattie 2-4-0WT No. 0263.
    1910 - 1922: 0-4-0ST No. 0458 *Ironside* (and 1/1926 - 5/1954).
    1924 - 1926: 0-4-0ST No. 734 *Clausentum* (and 2/1928 - 7/1936; 1940 - 9/1945).
    3/1938: "Terrier" No. 2678 trialled – unsuccessfully.
    1947: Ex-PDSW No. 756 *A.S. Harris*.
    1954 - 1959: B4 class 0-4-0T No. 30086.
    1959 - 3/1963: B4 class 0-4-0T No. 30089.
    3/1963 - 9/7/1967: USA class 0-6-0T No. 30072.

One of the many mentioned above is seen here in 1932: No. 734 *Clausentum*, a Hawthorn Leslie product (Works No. 2174 of 1890), built originally for Southampton Docks.

G. Coltas.

Plate 133: The sun shines down in June 1967, but the future is hardly bright, with only a month to go before regular steam operation leaves Southern metals for ever. Looking out from inside **Guildford's** roundhouse, with a shear-legs at left, we see BR Class 5 4-6-0 No. 73155 running onto the turntable and shed pilot No. 30072 waiting for access to the table, so it can shunt some ash wagons.

N. Hamshere

Plates 134 & 135: Steam's demise on 9th July 1967 was quickly followed by destruction of **Guildford** shed, to make way for parking spaces for the all-conquering motor car. The sad scene at centre dates from Autumn 1967, as 80 years of history comes crashing down. Bottom – you would never have known a shed had existed! Or would you? In 1970, the edge of Guildford's turntable pit was still to be seen, and even some of the 'infernal combustion' machines are history today. Such is progress!

Dr. T.A. Gough & N. Hamshere

Plate 136: **Hailsham's** single-road shed is visible on the left here, from the rear, in a unique c1875 view, looking south. The line from Polegate opened on 14th May 1849, with the shed following in 1858. Rails were extended to Eridge on 1st September 1880 and from then until October 1881, Hailsham shed covered four weekday return trips to Tunbridge Wells in addition to the Polegate shuttle. Closed soon after and subsequently demolished, the depot's west side wall actually existed until the station itself succumbed, following complete closure of the line on 9th September 1968.

S.C. Nash collection

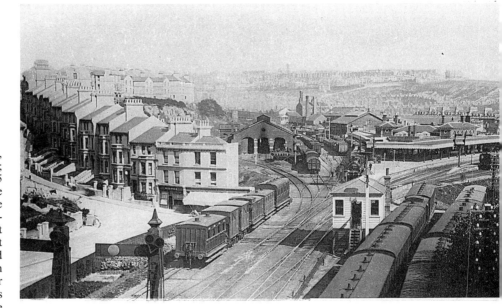

Plates 137 & 138: **Hastings** SER shed, seen from afar and in obscured close-up; the dates are 1893 (centre) and 1915 (bottom). This building dated from the 13th February 1851 opening of the line from Ashford. The route from Tunbridge Wells entered the station from 1st February the following year and with it came also the LBSCR, which had reached St Leonards (West Marina) on 7th November 1846 and then waited for completion of Bo Peep Tunnel to access Hastings. Until about 1870, when the Brighton company built its own permanent shed at St Leonards, it shared Hastings depot with the SER. Closure came in 1929, with replacement by a turntable and coaling stage sited just behind the camera's position in the top picture; that servicing facility was withdrawn after the 1957 dieselisation of London-Hastings services.

B. Matthews collection

Plate 139: The Cranbook & Paddock Wood Railway's branch to **Hawkhurst** was completed on 4th September 1893, and absorbed by the SECR in 1900. The terminus's two-road shed, seen on 30th March 1957, housed such types as Cudworth Class E 2-4-0s, Class O 0-6-0s, Class Q 0-4-4Ts, LCDR Class R1 0-4-4Ts, and even SER Class A 4-4-0 No. 157. Introduction of motor trains brought closure in 1931, but the shed remained for servicing, being 'fully' used, 25-28th January 1955, when Class E4 No. 32580 was marooned by a landslip at Horsmonden. Services were worked Hawkhurst-Goudhurst, with coal being supplied by a local merchant; crews came from Tonbridge by road. Final closure of the branch was on 11th June 1961, but the shed stands today, in private use.

T.J. Edgington.

Plate 140: The Hayling Island Railway opened its line in two stages. Havant to Langston was first, from 12th January 1865, and featured a temporary engine shed at Langston. Extension to the island came on 16th July 1867, with the single-road shed at the terminus actually being ex-Petworth, where it had served from 10th October 1859 to 15th October 1866. **Hayling Island's** wooden building closed in 1894 and was replaced by a simple coal stage, which is depicted here on 20th Septamber 1963, just over six weeks before final closure of the line.

W.T. Stubbs collection

Plate 141: **Haywards Heath** shed is thought to have opened in conjunction with the line from Keymer Junction to Lewes, on 1st October 1847. This rare view, dating from 1900, shows it in use as a goods shed, with part of the depot's substantial water tank just visible above the locomotive. When the change of use came about is not certain. An 1875 plan shows a track entering the shed where the goods office is positioned on the picture, passing a turntable and coal stage just outside. By 1890, the table had been moved to the other (north) end of the station and the shed converted as seen.

Lens of Sutton

Plates 142 & 143: **Hither Green** shed was built as part of the Southern's laudable programme of providing modern depot facilities, with opening on 10th September 1933. One of the author's favourite sheds, it could always be relied upon to turn up a surprise or two, often among the visitors from London Midland and Eastern Regions, that had worked in on cross-London goods. It is also recalled how difficult it was to catch Hither Green's 'King Arthur' 4-6-0s at home. The magnificently named *Sir Dodinas le Savage* (No. 30796), which was especially elusive, was finally 'nabbed' during a visit at 2am on a Saturday morning – 1950's train spotters were made of stern stuff! The depot is visible at top, on 22nd June 1954, with an 'Arthur' prominent – typical! Below is the coal stage, on 29th August 1951, with two veterans on display, a Class C 0-6-0 and Class E No. S1175, the latter soon to be withdrawn. Hither Green closed to steam in October 1961, thereafter serving diesels until recently and is now used as a PW depot.

B. Hilton & B.K.B. Green

Plate 144 & 145: Two scarce prints of the obscure little engine 'tank-shed' at **Holborn Viaduct**, provided for the station's opening on 2nd March 1874. The top picture dates from c1917, with that at centre being some 15 years later and showing what appears to be staff 'cabin' just right of the shed. Almost certainly there never was a formal allocation, this building and the cabin providing shelter for the pilot engine and its crew – and possibly for the occasional visiting locomotive. Date of closure is not known, but the building still stands, albeit minus the tank.

S.C. Nash collection

Plate 146: Another rare picture provides the only known glimpse of the single-road wooden shed at **Holsworthy**, just left of the train. Not seen are the coal stage and 40ft turntable outside the shed entrance. Opened on 30th January 1879, the depot's initial allocation was a Class 46 4-4-0T ("Ironclad"), from Okehampton, which had Nos 123, 124 and 130 at that time. Holsworthy was still a terminus when this photograph was taken, in 1895, with the extension to Bude not being completed until 10th August 1898. That was not the end though, as Holsworthy shed continued to house the branch goods engine until closure finally occurred in 1915, when the men and locomotive moved to Bude.

S.C. Nash collection

Plates 147 - 149: The top picture shows an ancient LBSCR Craven 'Standard Goods' engine shunting three withdrawn sisters at **Horley** in 1896. Built by the London & Brighton Railway, the shed and adjoining carriage shed (seen in the photograph) opened in 1841, with the locomotive depot also serving as a works. An allocation list of 1844 shows ten engines stationed at Horley, but the depot seems to have functioned only until the early 1860s whence it became a store for redundant and withdrawn engines. Then, by the mid-1890s it was in use as a goods depot, which led to it still being in existence today. At centre and bottom we see Horley shed in very recent times – the upper view of the north end taken on 13th July 1986, and the other of the south end, in June 1978, showing the pair of arched entrances made when the depot was converted for goods purposes. This remarkable survivor, now into its 148th year, seems bound to achieve its sesquicentenary. Let us hope so!

Lens of Sutton, S.C. Nash & Author

Plates 150 & 151: **Horsham's** first shed, a three-road affair beside the station, opened with the line from Three Bridges, on 14th February 1848. Further lines from Horsham were those to Petworth (10th October 1859), Shoreham (19th September 1861) Guildford (2nd October 1865) and Dorking (11th March 1876). The locomotive depot proved sufficient for all those workings, but eventually it needed replacement, this being effected about 1896 by provision of a ten stall part-roundhouse. Evidently, that building had been poorly planned as it needed extending very soon after and a further eight stalls were added during 1900/1. The top picture shows that work actually in hand, with the depot afterwards being sufficient for its average allocation of 30 engines. Duties decreased after the 2nd July 1938 electrification of the Three Bridges-Arundel route, but the shed continued to serve the remaining lines until closure in June 1964. It is seen below, late in life, on 21st September 1963.

F. Burtt/NRM & W.T. Stubbs collection

Plates 152 & 153: Above, M7 class No. 22 bustles away from **Ilfracombe**, up Morthoe Bank, in about 1913, its smoke neatly framing the Barnstaple & Ilfracombe Railway shed and 40ft turntable. The depot had opened with the line on 20th July 1874, housing at first the 'Ilfracombe Goods' 0-6-0s. Those engines, LSWR Nos 282-284, were designed specifically for the route, being delivered by Beyer Peacock in February 1873 and working over the Lymington branch until 'their' line was ready. Despite their "Goods" description, the 0-6-0s worked all services, up to 1900, and their replacement by 0-4-4Ts. Rebuilding of the station in 1928/9, caused the SR to close the shed and replace it with the concrete-built depot seen below from the rear, on 1st September 1950. Notice how the shed's site had been carved out of the hillside, particularly to accommodate the 65ft turntable, immediately below the photographer's position. This shed closed in September 1964 and the tortuous railway in October 1970, despite still substantial passenger carryings, albeit mostly during the summer.

S.C. Nash collection & A.R. Goult

Plate 154: Another incredible survivor today is **Kingston** (upon Thames), two-road depot, seen here in private use on 3rd February 1987. The shed opened on 1st July 1863 with the line from Twickenham, the station at Kingston remaining a terminus until completion of the 'Loop', on 1st January 1869. Earlier, on 3rd April 1866, Kingston saw services commence to Ludgate Hill and subsequent traffic grew so much that by March 1878, the shed's two engines were working 19 hours a day, with only $3^1/_2$ hours available for washouts, every eight days! That situation was alleviated in 1879, by delivery of new Class 46 4-4-0Ts, after which came Class 415 4-4-2Ts, O2 0-4-4Ts and finally, T1 0-4-4Ts, until the shed closed in 1907. It was then converted for goods use, which ensured its survival, to reach its present age of 126 years.

S.C. Nash

Plate 155: **Lancing Carriage & Wagon Works** opened in stages, 1908-1912. In June 1929, ex-SER crane tank No. 302 came to the works as No. 234S and stayed until October 1938, being joined in December 1932 by Class A1 "Terrier" No. 680S, a resident until June 1962. April 1937 saw arrival of Class A1x "Terrier" No. 515S, which remained up to August 1953, being replaced by another A1x No. DS681. In 1961, diesel shunters and USA 0-6-0Ts were trialled, but not before April and June 1963 did two USAs arrive – Nos DS235 and DS236, but they stayed until the works closed in 1965. All these engines were housed in a basic steel and asbestos shed, seen here on 30th March 1959, with residents Nos DS681 and DS680. Note DS681's 74A Ashford shedplate.

J.A. Sommerfield

Plate 156: **Launceston's** little corrugated iron shed opened with the railway from Halwill on 21st July 1886, services being extended to Delabole, then Wadebridge, on 15th October 1893 and 1st June 1895 respectively. The depot housed the engine off the last train from Okehampton, a duty that ceased after Nationalisation, although the turntable remained in use, with engines being housed in the nearby ex-GWR shed. The SR turntable expired in Summer 1963, after which 2-6-4Ts and 2-6-2Ts served, until the Western Region officially closed its Launceston engine facilities in September 1964. This scene is dated 7th June 1954.

E.V. Fry.

Plates 157 & 158: A very obscure shed, still standing today, is the LBSCR's single-road building at **Leatherhead**. Date of opening was apparently, 8th August 1859, with commencement of services from Epsom, to a station ½ mile north of the present edifice. The shed seems to have closed in 1874; certainly it does not appear in any of the author's allocation lists, which cover from 1896 to 1967. Subsequent to closure it served, among other things, as a chapel (!), school annexe and, for some time now, as a motor car repair shop. It is seen here in August 1986, from the north (above), showing the original arched entrance, and from the south (below), displaying the doorway made after locomotive use ceased. Notice too the pointed tops to the archway's windows, a legacy of the shed's days as a place of worship.

Author.

Plate 159: A view taken in about 1888 shows the Brighton platforms at **Lewes**, looking east, with the engine shed at right. The station was built in 1857, replacing the original 1846 terminus at Friar's Walk with, presumably, the shed serving until the Stroudley era, after which it was adapted for goods use. An 1873 plan shows the shed already converted, with a 35ft turntable retained in the junction of the Wivelsfield and Brighton lines, and a water tank on the north side of the latter, just west of the station. Little else is known about this locomotive depot, except that it was swept away in the station rebuilding programme of 1889.

NRM.

Plate 160: Alms houses form a backdrop to an inspiring vista at **Littlehampton**, c1933. This diminutive depot, a classic LBSCR design of the period, opened on 17th August 1863 and served as home for eight or nine engines until closed in 1937. That event was caused by the need to remodel the station for an electrification scheme, which was completed on 2nd July 1938. The shed survived though in somewhat altered condition, to enter private use, something that continues today.

S.C. Nash collection

Plate 161: This portait of LCDR 'Europa' class 2-4-0 No. 56 *America* includes the only glimpse of **Longhedge** roundhouse that has yet been discovered. Built as the LCDR's first major London depot, Longhedge was in fact a part-roundhouse of 40 radiating roads, half of them covered. It opened in February 1862, but had only a relatively short life, being closed 19 years later to make way for a huge, 16-road straight shed, known in later years as Stewarts Lane. This partial, but nonetheless valuable picture dates from 1876.
NRM

Plates 162 & 163: Two views, from far and near, of the branch terminus shed at **Lyme Regis**, taken on 23rd July 1958. One of the better known branch lines, it was opened by the Axminster & Lyme Regis Railway on 24th August 1903, initially being worked by the LSWR, and absorbed by it in 1907. The A&LRR provided a shed at Lyme Regis, but that was destroyed by fire in 1913, being replaced by the corrugated sheeting structure seen here. Initial power for the branch was provided by two ex-LBSCR "Terrier" 0-6-0Ts. They were LBSCR Nos 646 and 668 *Newington* and *Clapham* respectively, becoming LSWR Nos 734 and 735. Not a success, the "Terriers" were replaced by Class O2 0-4-4Ts in May 1907, these giving way 6½ years later to the Adams Radial tanks for which the line became so justly famous. Attempts were made to supersede those 4-4-2Ts by ex-LBSCR Class D1 0-4-2Ts, and even ex-GWR Class 1400 0-4-2Ts, but not until track improvements allowed use of ex-LMS Class 2 2-6-2Ts did the Adams Radials disappear. That was in July 1961, with the 2-6-2Ts serving until dieselisation brought about the shed's closure in November 1963.

B. Hilton

Plate 164: Opened on 12th July 1858, the Lymington Railway's branch had a shed at the **Lymington** terminus. The LSWR worked the line, absorbed it in 1878 and on 1st May 1884, extended it to Lymington Pier. Motive power was very varied during the 109 years of steam, with a 'Nelson' Class 2-4-0T at first, "Ilfracombe Goods" 0-6-0s, Adams Radials, O2s etc, right up to BR Standard designs. All were based at this little brick-built shed, seen here on 27th August 1951; the complete facilities are on view – no turntable was installed, that being at the branch junction station of Brockenhurst. Steam, and the shed, finished on 3rd April 1967 – BR's last steam branch – but the line lives on today, worked by electric multiple units.

A.R. Goult

Plate 165: An early shed, of Brighton & Chichester Railway origin (LBSCR), was that at **Lyminster** – or Arundel & Littlehampton – station, opened with the line from Worthing on 16th March 1846. Rails were extended to Chichester on 8th June 1846, but both station and shed continued to function until the Ford-Littlehampton branch came into use on 17th August 1863, at which point the entire Lyminster complex closed. Demolition did not occur though, and the long defunct, but privately occupied station and shed are seen here around the mid-1920s. Note that the locomotive depot had been of two-roads, for two engines – a classic **LBSCR** pattern of the period. Final fate of the building is not known.

S.C. Nash collection

Plate 166: The Southern Railway's only narrow gauge involvement was with the Lynton & Barnstaple Railway, a 1ft 11½in gauge line opened in 1898 and coming to the SR at Grouping. The new owner tried to keep that charming though anachronistic operation going, but eventually gave up and closed the whole route in 1935. There was a shed at each end of the line, with the least important being at **Lynton** – that very basic structure is seen here, from the rear, in about 1912.

Author's collection

Plate 167: **Maidstone's** SER station (West), saw two engine sheds, the first, of one road was brought into use on 25th September 1844 and served until 18th June 1856, when a three-road depot opened with the Strood line. It was a prominent shed for a time, with some 'star' locomotive turns to London, but its importance faded, and closure came in the SR's 1933 'spring clean'. Stabling, watering and turning facilities were retained until Maidstone's railways were electrified on 2nd July 1939. This picture, taken on 20th October 1936, shows the remains of the shed – offices, water tank, and two filled-in and one open pit roads; the Class C with 'SPL' target is not identified.

W.A. Camwell

Plate 168: Quite possibly built as an engine shed, but never used as such, was this building at **Margate Sands**, terminus of an SER branch from Ramsgate, opened on 1st December 1846. Plans from the 1870s onwards show that it had not been erected as a goods shed, because a separate structure for that purpose also existed. The plans show tracks going up to, but not into the building, and one at least has it designated as a stable – possibly its sole function? The terminus closed in 1926, with the adjacent yards eventually being made over for car parking. This 1948 photograph shows the 'mystery' building across that car park.

S.C. Nash

Plate 169: **Margate's** LCDR station (West) had a three-road locomotive shed between the mid-1860s and 1928. After closure, however, the SR maintained turning and watering facilities at the station, but on a different site. These remained in use until June 1961, even being made an 'official' stabling point, with coaling available in December 1960, following closure to steam of Ramsgate shed. This Indian Summer was captured on film on 4th February 1961, when six engines were present – there could be up to ten on Sundays. It is mildly surprising to recall that Sulzer and BRCW Type 2 diesels were common Kentish sights in those years – now they themselves are (almost) history!

S.C. Nash

Plates 170 & 171: The **LSWR** began extracting stone from **Meldon Quarry** in 1897, but it was 30 years before the operation became so big as to require stationing a shunting engine there. First was No. 225S, the ex-SER No. 313, a Manning Wardle 0-4-0ST built for duties at Folkestone Harbour. This was relieved for maintenance, as necessary, by B4 class No. 92 – or even an O2 – from Plymouth, with similar substitutes provided for Meldon's next 'permanent' resident, No. 500S. This was an ex-LCDR Kirtley Class T 0-6-0T (No. A607), which took over in March 1938 and was retired in December 1948. Its replacement was No. DS3152, an Adams Class G6 0-6-0T (No. 272), that was superseded by sister engine No. DS682 (ex-30238), in August 1960. Then, in December 1963, to see out the last years of steam, came No. DS234, a USA 0-6-0T, ex-30062. The Meldon pilot duty continues today, in the care of a Class 08 diesel shunter. Over the years, the pilots have been housed in two sheds, the first, of 1927 vintage, being of wood and corrugated iron construction. That is seen above in 1949, with Class O2 No. 30232 standing-in for the regular engine No. DS3152. The latter was, however, present when a second visit was made, on 1st June 1959 (below). It is evident that the first shed's desperate condition in 1949, had very soon after caused replacement by the concrete structure which still serves today and is, moreover, the only BR-built steam shed on any part of the former SR.

S.C. Nash

Plates 172 & 173: The small Sussex town of **Midhurst** had a complex railway history. There were two LBSCR lines, from Petworth and Chichester, completed on 15th October 1866 and 11th July 1881 respectively – in fact, the first was built by the Mid-Sussex & Midhurst Junction Railway, being worked by the LBSCR until absorption in June 1874. The MS&MJ had a single-road wooden shed at Midhurst and this is seen at top about 1906, looking very sorry for itself, a condition which caused its replacement in 1907. That new building is distantly seen at centre in the spring of 1935, twelve years after officially being closed by the SR; when it was finally pulled down is unclear. Two buildings left of the shed can be seen, the ex-LSWR station – that company's locomotive depot being just out of sight to the left. The train is arriving off the Chichester line, a working that would cease on 7th July 1935, the first of Midhurst's services to succumb. That continued until the final goods trains ran from Pulborough on 12th October 1964.

Lens of Sutton & B. Matthews collection

Plate 174: First tracks to enter **Midhurst** were those of the LSWR line from Petersfield, projected by the Petersfield Railway, which was absorbed by the LSWR on 22nd June 1863, and completed on 1st September 1864. A single-road shed was put up at the terminus, surviving the 12th July 1925 closure of that station, when all passenger services were concentrated at the ex-LBSCR station. However, closure of the LSWR shed did finally come in 1937, and it is seen here very soon after, with part of the roof already removed; demolition was quickly completed.

West Sussex County Council Library Service

Plates 175 & 176: The complicated story of the several rambling buildings at **New Cross** began on 1st June 1839, when the London & Croydon Railway (LBSCR from 27th July 1846) opened a roundhouse there – actually, the shed was octagonal in planform. That served until destroyed by fire on 14th October 1844, with replacement in the next year, by a three-road straight shed, referred to in later times as the "Croydon" shed. However, not all of the 'octagon' was lost as its turntable and radiating roads were incorporated into a repair shop, and are seen here above in 1947, still serving that purpose. Below, is one of the relatively scarce pictures of the "Croydon" or "Long" shed, as it was also known, c1946, near to the end of its working life. Just as well, seeing the condition it had descended to!

BR & B. Matthews collection

Plate 177: The dilapidated rear of "Croydon", with the two-road workshop visible through the arch. The date is 29th July 1947, a month after closure for running purposes, when engines seen were: Class I1X 4-4-2T No. 2003, Class D1/M 0-4-2T No. 2253 and Class B4X 4-4-0 No. 2067. **New Cross** continued as an "Engine Repair Depot" until final closure on 23rd May 1949.The thought of having to carry out such work, in such conditions, is daunting, but nevertheless, one of those hardy artisans has neatly hung up his jacket even though the slightest drop of rain would soak it. The likes of such men will never again be seen!

S.C. Nash

Plate 178: The third building at **New Cross** was another three-road straight shed, dead-end in pattern, with its entrances facing "Croydon" and separated from it by about 220 ft. Opened in 1848, this was another ill-starred structure, being blown down in a gale in 1863. This scene was taken the day after the storm and graphically shows how complete was the destruction, although most of the locomotives seem to have suffered only lightly. The building was quickly rebuilt to the same dimensions and layout, gaining the appellation of "Middle"; it was later extended to the rear.

S.C. Nash Collection

Plate 179: For number four of **New Cross** sheds, the LBSCR reverted in 1869 to a small octagonal 'roundhouse', tucked up into the south western corner of the site, adjacent to "Croydon's" repair shop. Why a building of such limited facility was put up is unknown, being able to house only the smallest tank engines – eg A1 class 0-6-0Ts and D1 class 0-4-2Ts. It rejoiced in the name of "Rooter" supposedly because of the proclivity of some of its inhabitants to hunt when in motion. "Rooter" is visible here on 4th March 1935 and it can be seen that dilapidation was not a post-war phenomenon!

H.C. Casserley

Plate 180: The last shed to be erected at **New Cross** was christened "New". A four-road through shed, opened in 1882, it stood north west of "Middle", with its north end roads terminating on a turntable. This picture, dating from the early 1900s, shows "New" in the distance and closer, the rebuilt "Middle" shed.

Author's collection

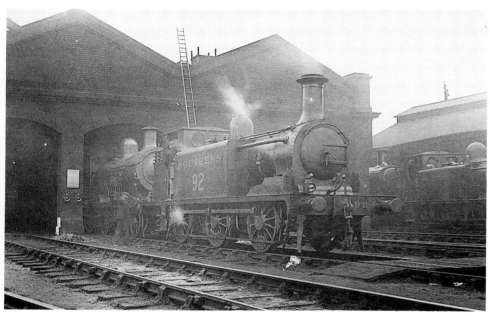

Plates 181 & 182: These two pictures feature **New Cross** "New" shed, that at centre dating from 18th May 1929, with shed pilot Class E1 No.B92 (ex-*Polesdon*) manoeuvring a 4-4-0. What is immediately apparent is that the building had been re-roofed, at a date unknown, losing its single-pitched gable in favour of twin pitches. Also visible, at right, is the wooden extension at the rear of "Middle"; once again, it is not apparent when this alteration was made. Below, is an interior shot, taken in 1951. As is obvious one roof pitch had already been removed and the building was serving as a store for surplus engines, a duty that ended very soon after. The chequered 118 year history of this intriguing locomotive depot came to an end with demolition in 1957.

G. Coltas & N. Sprinks

Plate 183: **Newhaven** was reached by the LBSCR on 8th December 1847, with a two-road engine shed being put up beside Harbour station. The depot provided motive power for main line services to London, and local trains to Seaford, Lewes and Brighton, these expanding to such an extent that by 1887, a larger shed had to be built. That four-road building appeared adjacent to Newhaven Town station and is depicted above, just after completion.

NRM

Plate 184: Not long after the harbour shed had been built it suffered a roof fire, which set a precedent of mishaps that was continued by its 1887 successor. For example, on 11th February 1889 it was reported that Class E1 0-6-0T No. 133 *Picardy* had run through the shed doors, while exactly five months later, Class C 0-6-0 No. 402 went through the depot's rear wall! That second accident cost £245 to rectify but no trace of the repair is visible in the superb interior view of **Newhaven** shed, dating from 1900.

F. Burtt/NRM

Plate 185: Guaranteed to bring sighs of nostalgia from all those 1950's "bashers" is this scene at **Newhaven** shed on 13th April 1958. The occasion was the running of the RCTS "Sussex Coast Limited" railtour, the working of which was shared by these four locomotives. It was also very significant in that it featured the last ever passenger duty by a British Atlantic-type engine, in this case No. 32424 *Beachy Head*. The author did not participate in the tour, but did join the RCTS three years after, so he can recognise several faces from their later participation in the many trips of those exhilarating days.

B. Hilton

Plates 186 & 197: **Newport,** Isle of Wight, saw its first Ryde & Newport Railway trains on 20th December 1875, the company putting up a two-road wooden shed there. The R&NR became part of the IWCR in 1887 and eventually Newport depot was working other lines, via Merstone, to Sandown and Ventnor West. In addition, from 10th September 1888 to 30th June 1913, it was responsible for services to Freshwater, over the FY&NR. Closure was at the quite early date of November 1957. A north end aspect is at top, around 1930, with Class O2 No. 30 taking water, while the centre view of the south end features a unique line-up. The year was 1947, just after Class E4 0-6-2T No. 2510 (second from left) arrived on the island for trials against the standard Class O2 0-4-4Ts. The E4 showed some success, but not enough, so it was returned to the mainland on 14th April 1949. It is here seen with an O2 at left and the island's two other types, ex-LBSCR A1x and E1 class 0-6-0Ts at right.

Author's collection & C.H.S. Owen

Plate 188: As mentioned above, FY&NR services were worked by the IWCR until the end of June 1913. From the next day the FY&NR worked its own trains and put up a shed at the **Newport** end of its line. The diminutive wooden building is distantly seen here in 1920 with resident FY&NR No. 1, a Manning Wardle 0-6-0ST (builder's No. 1555 of 1902), later named *Medina.* To help readers orient themselves, Newport station is behind the camera, while the shed is sited immediately east of Town Gate Viaduct.

S.C. Nash collection

FOCUS ON NINE ELMS

Plates 189 & 190: For many years one of the British Isles' biggest engine sheds, **Nine Elms** had small beginnings. First to open, on 21st May 1838, was a London & Southampton (LSWR from 1839) three-road shed at Nine Elms terminus, which was joined in 1849 by a six-road building. They lasted until 1865, and replacement by a seven-road through shed equipped with a turntable at each end. This was to be another short-lived affair, being superseded only eleven years later by a spacious semi-roundhouse of unusual design, with access from two turntables. That round shed is viewed from a distance above, at the turn of the century, a full panorama being obscured by a large double-sided coaling shed. That edifice is visible below in the early 1900s, giving good detail appreciation of the arched wagon road, roofed coaling roads, exterior and interior ashpits, and the unusual bi-directional water columns, two of which seem intended for use as engine-washing devices!

NRM & Lens of Sutton

Plates 191 & 192: Rarely photographed were the men of any engine shed's unglamorous non-footplate grades, so it is a pleasure to be able to present two such pictures here, both from the early years of this century at **Nine Elms.** At top we see what appears to be a turntable 'minder' and his hut. He is joined by a collection of colleagues of uncertain occupation, all getting in on the act, under the watchful eye of a bowler-hatted foreman. Below are the roundhouse shed's two turntables and distinctive office block/clock tower; labourers pause in their task of maintaining trackwork. Note that even in the confines of an engine shed, they have taken the precaution of posting a flagman – at front, right.

Lens of Sutton & B. Matthews collection

Plate 193: Continuing the **Nine Elms** phenomenon of short-lived adequacy, the roundhouse soon required relief, and this time the LSWR determined to provide a building which would be sufficient for more than a few years! The result was a commissioning in 1885, of this huge 15-road straight shed, which formed the prototype for six more large depots that would be erected during the succeeding 23 years. This shed had its own coal stage and turntable and was sited immediately west of the roundhouse, which henceforth, was relegated to housing Nine Elms' stud of tank locomotives. This photograph dates from just after opening.

NRM

Plate 194: An interior view of **Nine Elms'** 15-road building, dating from 12th June 1920 and showing how the ravages of time and use could affect such things as smoke trunking. Engines to be seen are M7 class No. 21, class 330 No. 0411, T1 class No. 365 and Adams Radial (class 0415) No. 0416.

H.C. Casserley

Plate 195: A scene looking across **Nine Elms,** from around 1916, shows part of the 15-road building and adjoining it, the 10-road straight shed put up in 1910, on the site of the roundhouse. It may be noted that the entrances of both sheds, christened "Old" and "New" respectively, were aligned to form a continuous 25-road edifice. Pictures of this are surprisingly rare though, hence inclusion of this less than ideal print. Note the immense 1885 coaling shed in the background.

Author's collection

Plate 196: A clearer picture of **Nine Elms** "New" shed, dating from 10th September 1949, when such confusions as BR-numbered locomotives attached to "Southern" tenders still pertained! Notice at left that the front of "Old" shed cannot be seen; the building's length was cut back following serious wartime damage. See also the 400 ton capacity mechanical coaling plant ordered by the LSWR, but actually completed in early SR times.

A.G. Ellis collection

Plate 197: How most of us remember **Nine Elms!** This trio of rebuilt Bulleid Light Pacifics was framed by the doorways of "New" shed on 27th July 1963. Their identities are: Nos 34025 *Whimple*, 34085 *501 Squadron* and 34060 *25 Squadron*.

T. Wright

Plate 198: The doyen Bulleid Pacific, No. 35001 *Channel Packet* makes ready on 14th July 1952, to haul Southern Region's No. 1 train – literally the "A.C.E."! The 65ft turntable was provided just before World War One, replacing a 50 footer installed with the "Old" shed. Originally manual in operation, the table seen here was subsequently converted to vacuum-tractor drive, enabling the locomotiveman to adopt his relaxed stance and enjoy the ride. Notice too that the tradition of a turntable 'minder's' hut had been continued (see *Plate 191*).

B.K.B. Green

Plates 199 & 200: Two pictures showing **Nine Elms** coalers in closer detail. At top we see the 1885 coaling shed, distantly visible in *Plate 195* and here in its final phase, de-roofed but still stocked with fuel despite its mechanised 1922/3 replacement behind – perhaps it was retained as a standby/supplementary facility? Standing on the ashpits on 20th May 1932 were rebuilt Class T14 ("Paddlebox") No. 462 and 'King Arthur' No. 783 *Sir Gillemere.* Eventually, the coal shed was removed, but visible traces existed until the end of Nine Elms shed, on 9th July 1967. The lower picture, from 8th March 1964, shows the remains of its supports while three Pacifics enjoy a rest from their labours. Notice the caterpillar-tracked grab crane used for ash clearing – normally, No. DS454, a rail-mounted, 2 ton capacity Grafton steam crane officiated.

G. Coltas & K. Fairey

Plates 201 & 202: Breakdown train facilities at **Nine Elms** saw employment of at least six steam, and one diesel crane over the years, with capacities rising from 15 tons, through 20, 36, and 45 tons, to reach 75 tons. Two of the early machines are seen here with, at the top, LSWR No. 1, a 15 tonner delivered in 1885 by the obscure firm of Dunlop & Bell. It is pictured c1890, before being renumbered 3, on replacement by a new No. 1. The D&B crane subsequently served at Eastleigh, Salisbury, Feltham and Bournemouth, before being withdrawn on 27th April 1946. Nine Elms' second crane No. 1 is pictured below, a Stothert & Pitt 20 tonner delivered in 1908. It sits on a roundhouse road, so the date must be soon after delivery – probably early 1909. This crane moved on in 1918, being based at Eastleigh and Bournemouth before withdrawal on 8th June 1963.

P. Tatlow collection

Plates 203 & 204: **Northam** shed may have opened with the LSWR's Southampton-Winchester section of line on 12th June 1839, or possibly in October 1840, when it is recorded that Driver Miller had been appointed (the first?) shed foreman. The depot closed in January 1903, but despite its 63 or 64 years of life and large size – 14 roads – it has yet to appear, complete, in any illustration. Why that should be must surely be put down to mischance, because photographers were certainly active at the shed, as these two prints show. The upper view is of Class T9 No. 706 on an 'up' special in 1899, passing Northam's west end, just visible at left. Below, from an unfortunately much deteriorated negative, comes this c1890 portrait of Beattie 'Lion' class 0-6-0 No. 13, with part of the north end of Northam shed building in the background. The engine, incidentally, was formerly named *Orion* and is seen as modified by Adams. It went to the Duplicate List in April 1893, to be withdrawn in July 1899.

S.C. Nash collection & H. Garratt collection

Plate 205: The last of the SR's big concrete-built sheds, **Norwood Junction** came into use in 1935, allowing closure of a life-expired shed at nearby West Croydon. The purpose of the depot was to provide goods and shunting engines for the yards in the Norwood/Selhurst area, which it did quietly and unspectacularly for just under 29 years, to closure in January 1964. This photograph was taken from the shed entrance footbridge on 6th September 1959, and graphically displays all the depot's facilities except the turntable, which was sited at the rear of the building. As can be seen, the coal stage pilot engine was one of the early types of diesel shunter. No. 15201 was designed in SR days by Bulleid; several other, later sisters may also be observed.

T.J. Edgington

Plate 206: A scene epitomising all that was fascinating about London's steam railways. We are standing at the 'neck' of **Norwood Junction** shed yard, deep in Southern Region territory, about 1955, when rattling round the corner from Bromley Junction comes London Midland Region 8F class No. 48074 from 1A Willesden shed. It is hauling a transfer goods that will be left in a nearby yard, whence the 2-8-0 will visit the Southern shed for turning and servicing, before setting off again for its home on the north side of the River Thames.

Author's collection

Plates 207 & 208: Two pictures illustrating some change over the years at **Okehampton,** high up on the edge of Dartmoor. The railway first reached the town in the early 1870s, but no shed was provided until 1894. That little single-road wooden building was consumed by fire in 1920 so the LSWR quickly replaced it with a concrete-built shed, which is seen above on 3rd August 1928, with the 50ft turntable, water crane and coal platform also on view. Class 0395 0-6-0 No. E029 has just had its fire cleaned and now some poor fellow has the job of heaving all that hot ash into a wagon. The increasing size of locomotives eventually required a larger turntable, so a 70ft version was installed right at the end of the SR's existence. It is shown below on 26th August 1959 with Class N No. 31849 aboard, behind which may be seen the new coaling stage provided at the same time as the table. Okehampton depot was closed by the Western Region in June 1965.

B. Matthews collection & K. Fairey

Plates 209 & 210: One of the only two sheds of SECR origin, **Orpington** opened in 1901 as part of the Joint Managing Committee's plans to eradicate antiquated engine facilities – Bickley being a near example. However, the two-road shed was destined to have a working life of only a quarter of a century, closing as part of an early SR electrification scheme. That scheme was completed on 12th July 1925, but the shed did not cease to operate until the following year, as the upper photograph shows it still in use, on 14th February 1926. Such a recent building was bound to survive though, and Orpington shed still serves BR today as office premises for the Civil Engineer; the lower illustration depicts it in June 1977.

H.C. Casserley & Author

Plate 211: The main engine shed of the 1 ft 11$^1/_2$ in gauge Lynton & Barnstaple Railway was at **Pilton Yard,** Barnstaple, opened in 1898. Independent until the Grouping, the L&B's Southern management lasted 12 years, until the inevitable closure came in 1935. This picture of the two-road depot and adjoining carriage sheds was taken just prior to the end, with 2-4-2T No. 762 *Lyn,* making ready to haul one of the last trains. Dismantling of the railway and sale of materials followed soon after, but Pilton Yard engine shed is still standing today, in private use.

A.B.Macleod/NRM

Plate 212: Class O2 No. 195, marked 'S.W.R', stands outside **Plymouth Friary** engine shed about 1897, providing the scantest but only known glimpse of the two-road, stone-built depot opened with the terminus, on 1st July 1891. This little four-engine building shared Plymouth duties with the 1876 shed at Devonport (see *Plate 69),* until both were superseded in 1908 by a new, much larger Friary shed. Also just seen here, behind the engine, is the depot's coal platform which appears largely to have remained after the shed was replaced by – or incorporated into – a goods shed. Look at the young chap standing stiffly to attention by No. 195's front buffer – one wonders what life held for him in late Victorian times, and after?

S.C. Nash collection

Plate 213: **Plymouth Friary's** replacement shed was this substantial three-road building, put up at Lucas Terrace, a short way out of the terminus. This view of the east end dates from 15th June 1926, when the 18 year old depot was still in original condition, except perhaps for newly replaced smoke vents; the coaling stage and turntable were behind the camera. Locomotives prominent are Class L11 4-4-0 No. E172 and Class N 2-6-0 No. A865.

H.C. Casserley

Plate 214: A scene from inside **Plymouth Friary** on 30th August 1945. The ravages of time and the just-ended Second World War have had their effect, with windows having their panes either blacked-out or blasted out! The Class B4 0-4-0T No. 91 was one of several of its type allocated to Friary for various shunting turns. Those fitted with spark-arresters, such as this example, were primarily used on the Oreston Timber Yard pilot duty.

H.C. Casserley

Plate 215: **Plymouth Friary's** west end, late in the afternoon of 25th September 1961 with the engine hoist prominent. Several changes are apparent. First, the building's roof and glazed gables had been replaced by corrugated sheeting – probably in BR times. Second, the shed was transferred to the Western Region in 1958, by which time the 204 hp diesel shunters visible had superseded such types as the B4 tanks. As may be observed though, Bulleid Pacifics still held sway at the time and the author recalls that the four members of the type allocated to Friary: Nos 34011 *Tavistock,* 34012 *Launceston,* 34013 *Okehampton* and 34021 *Dartmoor,* were particularly tough nuts for a Londoner to crack! But, their days too were numbered and the shed finally closed in May 1963, to be demolished and replaced by private development.

W.T. Stubbs collection

Plates 216 & 217: **LBSCR** trains first entered through **Polegate** when the Brighton to St Leonards line opened, on 27th June 1846, with junctions for Eastbourne and Hailsham branches being added on 14th May 1849. During 1859/60 Polegate station was re-modelled and it was probably at that time when an engine shed was put up, a single-road tank-shed with 36ft turntable outside the entrance. (From plans the shed would seem to have been virtually identical to such a building at Three Bridges, a good side view of which is seen in *Plate 289.*) Quite what duties Polegate depot undertook is not clear, with sheds at Hailsham and Eastbourne handling traffic over those routes. Anyway, in 1881 the Hailsham branch was realigned, that deviation cutting through Polegate engine shed, which was accordingly reduced in length by a half. Whether the depot had already been closed by 1881, or if it closed then, or later, is not known. These two views from the south show the truncated building – above, in the late 1920s and below, in August 1962. Obvious changes are that water softening apparatus and miscellaneous huts had been removed between those dates and the LBSCR signal gantry had given way to one of SR pattern. In 1962 Bulleid Pacific No. 34019 *Bideford* was heading north off the Eastbourne line, with a holiday train for the Midlands, while rebuilt sister No. 34089 *602 Squadron* waited to back down onto a similar working.

S.C. Nash collection & S.C. Nash

Plate 218: Another of those building-less stabling and servicing points used by locomotives between duties was **Portsmouth, Burnaby Road,** situated betwixt Town and Harbour stations. Seen resting there around the year 1906 was Class E5 No. 576 *Brenchley,* together with part of the 55ft turntable and piles of ash; up to five engines could be found there at times. Opening and closing dates are uncertain.

B. Matthews collection

Plates 219 & 220: Last of all SER engine sheds built was **Purley,** opened in 1898 and enabling closure of small depots at, Caterham and Kingswood. A three-road northlight roofed building, Purley's first inmates were Class 118 2-4-0 Nos 68, 71, 221 and 229 these later being supplanted mainly by Class H 0-4-4Ts. No 512 of that type was on view above, on 22nd May 1926, when Purley was photographed from the south. Of the depot's facilities, the water tank is clearly seen, but a 50ft turntable is out of picture to the left and the coal stage is hidden between the GWR 5-plank wagon and locomotive. Electrification brought closure in 1928, but the building was adapted for other use and survives today in excellent order. This is evident from the scene below, taken on a snowy 23rd February 1986; the shed's present purpose is a BR repository for legal archives.

H.C. Casserley & J.A. Sommerfield

Plate 221: **Although** given 'official' status by the LCDR, **Ramsgate Harbour** locomotive depot never had a building. However, there were standing and watering facilities, with coaling from wagons and turning via the turntable installed at the terminus' 'buffer-stop' end. This elevated view of the station dates from just after the Grouping – on a Bank Holiday no doubt, to judge by the crowds! The small engine yard is at right, with the water tank and coal wagons visible; there was additional standing room immediately below the camera's left hand. The entire branch into the terminus, which was opened by the Herne Bay & Faversham Railway on 5th October 1863, and absorbed by the LCDR in 1871, closed on 2nd July, 1926.

H. Garratt collection

Plates 222 & 223: The first engine shed in **Ramsgate** was that of the SER, sited by Town station and opened on 13th April 1846. It is depicted in these two pictures – distantly (left) from the station, in about 1919, and close up, some 30 years earlier (right), when Class 118 2-4-0 No. 247 was in residence. This type was staple power at that time, being replaced in the late 1890s by Class B 4-4-0 for working such trains as the prestige "Kent Coast Express", 7.45 and 7.55 am from Margate Sands to Cannon Street; 4.47 and 4.57 pm returns. Ramsgate Town station and shed closed on 2nd July 1926.

Author's collection & B. Matthews collection

Plates 224 & 225: Two elevated views of the SR's six-road concrete engine shed at **Ramsgate,** brought into use between 1928 and 1930. At top, the depot is seen from the coaling tower c1935, while below, a 1931 print shows that coaling plant, turntable and spacious yard. Visible in the distance is the station built along with the shed, but notice that the large carriage shed glimpsed above, had not then been erected. Steam lasted for 32 years at Ramsgate, being banished at the end of 1960. At that time the building was incorporated into a depot for housing and servicing the replacement electric multiple units and as such, it remains today.

Author's collection and B. Hilton collection

Plates 226 & 227: **Ramsgate's** SR shed had a well known landmark in its stationary boiler locomotive. That above, Class O 0-6-0 No. A98, seen c1935, served the purpose for almost 24 years; November 1929 to mid-1953. It was superseded by Class D 4-4-0 No. 31501, depicted here partly interred, on 15th April 1956. It was about that time when the author first visited depot 74B, clutching his Ian Allan *ABC of Southern Region Locomotives*. Still naive enough not to realise that engines did not live forever, the author well remembers the righteous indignation felt when he could not underline No. 31501 in his spotter's 'bible'. The reason was simple – the "ABC" was a 1956 edition, printed three years after the D had been withdrawn from capital stock! Ah, the innocence of youth!

G. Coltas & T. Wright

Plates 228 & 229: The history of the Southern's shed at **Reading** is a bit of a puzzle. The Reading, Guildford & Reigate Railway commenced services from Reading to Farnborough on 4th July 1849, extended to Guildford nearly seven weeks later, and reached Redhill on 15th October 1849, thereby establishing a well known and long-lived cross-country route. The SER absorbed the RG&RR in 1852, and on 9th July 1856 LSWR trains commenced running into Reading, that company stationing an engine there until Grouping. During this time a three-road locomotive depot appeared, very likely around 1853, because it was virtually identical in layout and size to Redhill shed (see next page), which was built in that year. The only differences were that Redhill had arched entrances against Reading's square-topped (which could originally have been curved of course), and positioning of coaling and turning facilities. So, was there a Reading shed prior to the 1850s? Given what is known about Redhill's earliest days it seems unlikely, but evidence either way has yet to be found. The picture of the shed's east end, above, dates from 8th October 1949 with U1 class No. 31898, while that below, showing the west end, comes from about 1960; note that BR had re-roofed the building in the intervening period. Closure came in 1965, with subsequent demolition and redevelopment of the site.

T.J. Edgington & B. Matthews collection

Plate 230: **Redbridge Permanent Way Depot** was set up by the LSWR in 1884. A resident pilot engine was employed, being housed in its own shed which, judging by the building style seen in this c1966 photograph, dated from opening of the works. Class USA tank No. DS233 was the last steam engine to serve the PW depot, but details of its predecessors are sketchy. What is known is that diminutive Class C14 0-4-0T No. 77S/DS77 (ex-LSWR No. 745), was at Redbridge from October 1927 until December 1957. It is also known that when the C14 was under maintenance, substitute power was provided in the shape of an O2 class 0-4-4T or, in the late 1930s, 0-4-0ST No. 734 *Clausentum* (see *Plate 132*). The date of closure of this little shed is not known, but Redbridge depot continued to function until as recently as March 1989.

S.C. Nash collection

Plate 231: As mentioned in the caption to *Plates 228 & 229,* **Redhill** SER shed opened in 1853 (May), having been authorised on 23rd September 1852. Prior to that, locomotives had stood in the open, including those stored awaiting works, eg 16 engines on 30th June 1852. Redhill is seen here from the south in the 1920s, virtually as built, with a typical Sunday 'full house'. Of the depot's facilities, the coal stage and turntable are out of sight to the left – the former's wagon ramp is visible in the distance.

Lens of Sutton

Plate 232: A close-up of **Redhill's** southern end on 28th June 1947, showing little change from some 20 years earlier, as seen in the preceding Plate; even the doors are intact – no mean achievement! However, electricity cables spanning the entrance, and a few outbuildings at left and right are obvious additions, as are the Class Q locomotives – Nos 538 and 537. They and Class D 4-4-0 No. 1728, seem reluctant to step out into the sunshine!

H.C. Casserley

Plate 233: Southern glory! Impeccably maintained Class D No. 1748 poses with Class H No. 1512, and a proud-looking shed foreman, by **Redhill's** coal stage, sometime in the early 1930s.

Author's collection

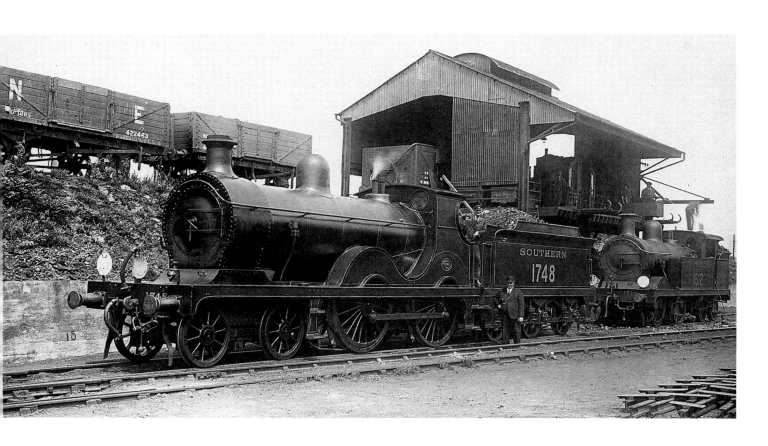

Plate 234: Another view of **Redhill's** southern aspect, this time from August 1964, showing how **BR** had altered the building in 1950. Gone are the arched entrances and tiled gabled roof, the latter being replaced by the standard steel and asbestos sheeting, with a brick screen at the north end. It is only ten months before the depot's closure, with the end of steam thereabouts, so the residents have a care-worn look. That also applies to Canklow shed's Class B1 No. 61313, which in June, had failed on the Edinburgh-Lewes vans. The Thompson 4-6-0 was eventually put right by Redhill's fitters at the end of September and worked an empty stock train to Brighton, two passenger trips to Reading and finally, a special freight to Streatham Common, whence it ran light to Cricklewood, then home to Canklow.

S.C. Nash

Plates 235 & 236: Opened from Robertsbridge to Tenterden on 29th March 1900, the Rother Valley Railway became the more well known Kent & East Sussex Railway in 1904, a year before the the Tenterden-Headcorn section came into use. Motive power for the whole route was based at **Rolvenden,** where the original "Dutch Barn" style of engine shed is seen above, soon after opening. Such a flimsy-looking structure was bound not to last and sure enough, by 28th December 1953 below, Rolvenden shed presented a very different aspect. Whether the first depot had been completely replaced, or merely rebuilt is not clear – neither is the date of any such alteration. The K&ESR remained independent until coming into **BR** in 1948, after which the State system maintained passenger services to 4th January 1954. From that date the shed closed and was demolished, but it was not until 12th June 1961 that the last section of the K&ESR, from Robertsbridge to Tenterden, finally succumbed. Today of course, the line has partially been re-opened by a private preservation company.

Author's collection & E.V. Fry

Plate 237: Isle of Wight Railway trains first ran between Ryde and Shanklin on 23rd August 1864, the line being extended to Ventnor on 10th September 1866. Engines were housed in a two-road shed at **Ryde,** that serving until 1874, when a larger building was opened on the opposite side of the station. However, a developing Ryde Works incorporated the first engine shed and it survives today, in use mainly as a store. It is seen here on 23rd May 1964, with Class O2 No. 17 *Seaview* under repair outside. The ancient 5 ton hand crane was numbered DS425 (SR 425S).

J.A. Sommerfield

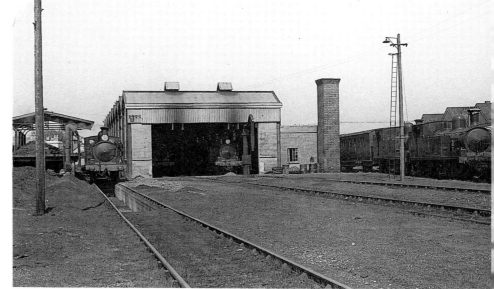

Plates 238 & 239. Photographs of **Ryde's** second shed are very scarce, which is surprising as the two-road building was in use up to 1930. In that year the SR opened a much larger concrete and asbestos two-road depot immediately west of the station, seen in the centre picture on 21st April 1957: Notice the brace of stored O2s – a standard IoW practice during the lightly trafficked winter months. In the lower view, No. W17 *Seaview* is again observed, when Ryde's third shed was only two years old, and veterans such as No. W16 *Wroxall* were still in service. She had been built by Beyer Peacock (builder's No. 1141 of 1872), for the IWR, and would be withdrawn and scrapped in the following year.

T.J. Edgington & G. Coltas

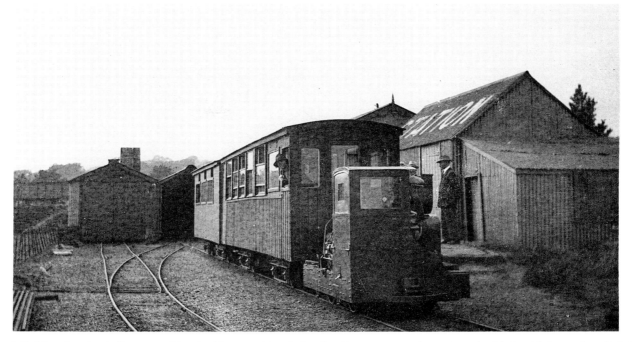

Plate 240: Use of author's licence enables the 3ft gauge Rye & Camber Tramway to gain an entry in this book! Opened on 13th July 1895 from Rye to Camber Golf Links, the R&CT was extended exactly 13 years later to Camber Sands. The company employed Bagnall 2-4-0T *Camber* at first, housed in a shed at **Rye,** seen here at left. The picture dates from 1927, two years after steam had given way to the petrol-engined Kent Construction built 'device' visible in the station. Services were run until 1939, when the military took over for the period of the war. After the war's end, the line was handed back to its owners but was in such a bad state it never re-opened; official winding up of the company is thought to have taken place in 1946.

B. Matthews collection

Plate 241: A relatively obscure shed was that at **St Helens,** near Bembridge, Isle of Wight, on the IWR branch opened on 27th May 1882. Services were worked for the first 35 years by *Bembridge,* a Manning Wardle 0-6-0T (builder's No. 517 of 1875), bought from the contractor which built the line and housed in this shed beside St Helens dock. When *Bembridge* went away to war in 1917, it is possible the shed then closed, to be taken over for other purposes. Certainly by 1937, when this picture was taken, the depot had a long-closed look and was being used as a carpentry workshop, with a very formally attired artisan at work outside. Note his bicycle propped up against the sleeper-built coal platform and the '1882' date on the 1,600 gallon water tank. This building still stood in 1949, but as the whole line was closed on 21st September 1953, it is reasonable to assume the shed was removed around that time.

T. Cooper collection

FOCUS ON ST LEONARDS

Plate 242: There is uncertainty about the opening date of the first LBSCR shed at **St Leonards** (known to that railway as "Hastings"). The Brighton, Lewes & Hastings Railway was completed to St Leonards (West Marina) on 7th November 1846 and it is probable that some sort of engine facilities were provided, pending the boring of Bo Peep Tunnel and the LBSCR's access to Hastings SER shed. St Leonards' first locomotive depot appears on the 1873 issue of the Ordnance Survey and is thought to have been brought into use a year or so before then. Only one photograph has been traced so far, an 1892 general view with the shed appearing in the distance, as is evidenced here. The two-road building was single-ended and had a layout and physical looks that bore a close similarity to a number of early LBSCR depots. So, it is possible that St Leonards was of a vintage prior to the early 1870s – but this matter is unclear.

Lens of Sutton

Plate 243: By the late 1890s **St Leonards'** two-road shed was no longer adequate, so in 1898 it was superseded by a four-road northlight depot on virtually the same site. The eastern end of the shed is hazily depicted here when about seven years old and Class B4 No. 58 *Kitchener* was having its boiler lifted by 15 ton crane No. 16, normally based at Brighton. Notice that only three of the shed's roads were accessible from the east.

Author's collection

Plate 244: This magnificent view of **St Leonards'** west end dates from about 1900, with Class C 0-6-0 No. 422 and Class **B2** No. 209 *Wolfe Barry* identified. On 19th July 1903, oil-burning Class **B2** No. 202 *Trevithick* would cause a fire that did little damage to 'himself', but incurred the **LBSCR** a considerable roof repair bill.

F. Burtt/NRM

Plate 245: Another beautifully posed photo at **St Leonards** has B2 class No. 315 *J. Gay* (formerly *Duncannon*), standing on the depot's 50ft turntable, circa 1907. These graceful 4-4-0s — or more correctly, the B2x rebuilds — held sway at St Leonards until the 1929 closure of Hastings ex-SER shed. That caused an influx of ten Class F1 4-4-0s which took over the B2x duties, including the London turns.

F. Burtt/NRM

Plates 246 & 247: As with most northlight roofs that at **St Leonards** had, in time to be replaced by something more substantial. BR undertook the work during 1949, as the top picture shows – also giving a good idea of the yard layout around the turntable and coaling plant. By 20th September 1950, below, re-roofing had been completed long enough for smoke to start staining the brick end screens that hid the four longitudinal steel and asbestos pitches.

B. Matthews collection & B. Hilton

Plate 248: Another unique, but sadly poor photograph portrays the little known shed at **Salisbury (Milford)**. This hipped roof, two-road building was put up for the opening of the line from Bishopstoke on 27th January 1847. Next, on 1st May 1857, LSWR trains started to run to Salisbury from Andover, using Milford terminus (necessitating a reversal), until Fisherton LSWR station opened in 1859. (The GWR had started running into its Fisherton terminus, from the west, in April 1858.) At that point, Milford station was turned over to goods use, including some time after, the engine shed. In that condition it remained for many years, as this picture is purported to date from 1934. When Milford shed was removed has yet to be discovered.

S.C. Nash collection

Plate 249: On opening, **Salisbury Fisherton** station was provided with a three road brick-built engine shed at its western end. Pictures of that building are hard to come by, but this portrait of Class 0395 No. 509 gives a good impression of what the shed's western end looked like on 26th September 1900.

F. Burtt/NRM

Plate 250: Plans from 1880 show two roads passing through the rear (east) wall of **Salisbury Fisherton** shed, but it would seem that when built, the depot was single-ended in style. Possible evidence of this later alteration comes from a 1900 picture of Class T9 No. 709 with, at left, a glimpse of a steel lintel over a square eastern entrance – quite different to the arched doorways of the opposite end.

F. Burtt/NRM

Plate 251: There was a second building at **Salisbury Fisherton,** a three-road wooden structure, sited at the immediate south east corner of the brick shed. Also having two roads 'through' (at the western end), it had been built about 1890, intended only as a temporary annexe, pending a move of the LSWR's entire Salisbury locomotive depot to a new location. Like its 1859 neighbour, the wooden shed was most camera-shy but this very acceptable east end picture from 1900 does give a good idea of the building's appearance; the pair of 4-4-0s are actually standing on the tracks at the rear of the first shed. Both Fisherton buildings were demolished soon after the 1901 opening of a new engine shed about half a mile to the east.

F. Burtt/NRM

Plate 252: **Salisbury's** spacious ten-road locomotive depot was about 30 years old when this wintry scene was captured. A great improvement over the previous cramped quarters by the station, the shed was more in keeping with its important role as the engine-change point for West of England trains. All through its existence it sported a sizeable stud of express passenger types and even had a locomen's dormitory, positioned somewhat insensitively beneath the depot's water tank, as at Eastleigh. By the time this picture was taken, the initial 55ft turntable had been replaced by a 65 footer, but generally, the building remained in its original condition for over 50 years.

A.B. Macleod/NRM

Plate 253: Last of the SR's first batch of 15 Class S15s, a sunbathed No. E837 was but three months old when this picture was taken, on 28th April 1928. Fine detail of the LSWR's glass-gabled sheds is evident, even down to the decorative finials atop the roof ridges. Despite the generally good building design though, maintenance was a constant occupation (as with any pattern of engine shed), this being evidenced by the ladder at extreme right, with nearby 'roofless' and re-painted smoke vents.

H.C. Casserley

Plates 287 & 288: **Three Bridges'** first LBSCR engine shed most likely came into use with completion of the line to Horsham, on St Valentine's Day 1848. Additional duties were incurred when the branch to East Grinstead opened on 9th July 1855, but for many years the shed never had more than about six engines outstationed from Horsham, with one sub-shedded at East Grinstead. For example, an 1896 allocation list shows the following:

Three Bridges – Class E1 Nos 102/4/10; D1 Nos 258/75/94.

East Grinstead – Class D1 No. 233.

In the top view we see a posed picture of Three Bridges station, from the south, with the shed just visible at left, on a lower level. The awkward and cramped site precluded provision of facilities. They were located in the fork of the Haywards Heath and Horsham lines and comprised a 45ft turntable sited outside a tank-shed, that had one road entering from the north; another spur ran beside a coal platform. Below is a close-up of Three Bridges' two-road shed, with a pair of Class D1s taking their ease between duties. Both these pictures date from around 1905.

B. Matthews collection & S.C. Nash collection

Plate 289: The tank-shed at **Three Bridges** is displayed here in 1900, nine to ten years before it apparently had a brief moment of glory. Expansion of the station commenced in 1909, utilizing space on the 'up' side, including that occupied by the engine shed. Accordingly, a replacement had to be constructed and an Ordnance Survey plan of 1911, surveyed in 1910, shows the station shed gone but the new depot not yet complete. However, the tank-shed had gained the appellation "Engine Shed" and been converted from dead-end to through in pattern, with the track exiting the south wall and leading to the marshalling yard. So, it seems that for a period of up to a year, the edifice seen above may have 'bridged the gap' between closure of Three Bridges' old shed and opening of the new.

F. Burtt/NRM

Plate 290: Sited on the south side of the Horsham line, **Three Bridges'** (third?) shed is visible here from the north, about 1929, with a full house and pumping engine boiler obviously in use. The large number of locomotives is indicative of how the depot's importance had increased – so much so in fact that it eventually attained a status separate from Horsham.

S.C. Nash collection

Plate 291: A distant southerly view of **Three Bridges**, from 24th June 1954, shows a stored 0-6-2T 'out in the park', the coal stage immediately left of the main building and the engine hoist – the latter spanning a spur leading to a 60ft turntable, unseen at right. The shed passed out of locomotive use in June 1965, but saw several more years employment as a wagon shop, before being demolished.

B. Hilton

Plate 292: If one discounts two earlier sheds built for absorbed companies, **Tonbridge** was the SER's first locomotive depot, opening on 26th May 1842. Sited in the fork of the Ashford and (later) Hastings lines, Tonbridge originally comprised a three-road dead-end shed facing east, with a small carriage shed placed at right angles immediately by the depot's south west corner. By the 1880s Tonbridge had passenger services to Ashford, Hastings, Maidstone and Redhill, mostly hauled by a sizeable allocation of "Ironclad" 2-4-0s. To accommodate them the original building had been lengthened and one track taken 'through', and a longer three-road section added on the south side. That building was of the through type, but initially only just, with the tracks terminating just out of the eastern end. The extension covered the site of the carriage shed which may, or may not, have been incorporated, so a new carriage building was put up on the south side. Lastly, a 42ft turntable was positioned by the shed's north west corner. There matters rested until the turntable was moved onto the second carriage shed's site, as may be seen on the right of this 17th July 1926 scene taken from the west. The coal stage stands out of picture to the left, in the turntable's first position.

H.C. Casserley

Plate 293: The three roads of **Tonbridge's** second section were eventually extended eastwards, through an area that came to be called "The Gardens". It is from there that we see an historic but sad occasion – 17th June 1962 and the last day of Tonbridge's steam allocation. Identified engines are 'Schools' class No. 30915 *Brighton,* BR Standard 2-6-4Ts Nos 80037, 80066 and 80065 and, with "The End" chalked over the smokebox door, Class N No. 31880.

B.I. Fletcher

Plate 294: Another vista from the east, this time on 21st September 1963, finds **Tonbridge** hosting at least four steam locomotives, over 15 months after losing its own allocation; such visitations would persist for a further 15 months! More clearly seen is the brick-screened, steel and asbestos roof applied by **BR** in the early 1950s. Note the shorter section at right – the original building – had been reduced to two roads, a move necessary to accommodate the diesel fuel tanks, given the cramped nature of the site.

W.T. Stubbs collection

Plate 295: Formal 'closure' of **Tonbridge** occurred in January 1965, with subsequent demolition, but even that was not the end. This picture dates from 30th June 1968 – one of those periodic "Go Slow" days that **BR** used to suffer more frequently than of late. Still standing was the shed's south wall, which included offices and stores in its fabric. The depot roads were also still in situ and among the residents were diesel shunter No. 15222, E5001, "Hastings" 6-car diesel electric unit No. 1007, "Tadpole" diesel electric unit No. 1201, D6582, D6591 and E6046. Given that all this 'power' could still be found, is it not therefore strange (some would say typical!) that Tonbridge's diesel fuelling facility had been removed? Stabling of diesel locomotives did not cease for several more years.

B.I. Fletcher

Plate 296: Tracks from the North Devon Railway terminus at Bideford were extended to **Torrington** on 1st July 1872, the LSWR erecting a single-road, mainly wooden engine shed at the new railhead. That building is seen here, 65 years on and much in its original condition, except for removal of a 40ft turntable from outside the shed entrance. The table's demise indirectly followed the 27th July 1925 extension of the line, as the North Devon & Cornwall Light Railway, to Halwill Junction. To work between Halwill and Barnstaple a trio of 460 class 4-4-0s came to Torrington, being superseded by Class E1/R 0-6-2Ts in 1928, thereby rendering the turntable redundant. Those tank engines held sway for many years, together with M7 0-4-4Ts, until LMS design 2-6-2Ts arrived, in the 1950s. They and the occasional M7 then operated from Torrington until closure of the shed in 1959.

W.A. Camwell

Plate 297: **Tunbridge Wells West's** second engine shed replaced a two-road East Grinstead, Groombridge & Tunbridge Wells Railway (LBSCR) depot, opened on 1st October 1866 and sited to the south of the station. Further traffic developments were:
1867 – goods traffic extended through tunnel to SER station.
3/8/1868 – Uckfield to Groombridge opens.
1876 – passenger traffic extended to SER station.
1/9/1880 – Hailsham to Eridge (Groombridge) opens.
1/10/1888 – Oxted to Groombridge opens.
  All of which made Tunbridge Wells West a pretty busy place and it was not long – 1890/1 – before rebuilding of the station caused a new engine shed to be erected at the west end. It is seen here when a year or two old, with Craven 2-4-0 No. 207 *Freshwater* as one of the few residents.

Lens of Sutton

Plate 298: A very nice interior shot of **Tunbridge Wells West,** dating from c1900, again reminds us of the high standards of cleanliness maintained by the LBSCR for all its locomotives – and their sheds. Stroudley Single No. 337 *Yarmouth* holds centre stage, preceded by D1 class No. 257 *Brading,* and succeeded by D3 class No. 372 (formerly *Amberley*), and two more D1s.

F. Burtl/NRM

Plates 299 & 300: Two pictures showing transition at **Tunbridge Wells West.** The interesting view above dates from October 1950 and commemorates the twilight of ex-LBSCR passenger tank engines. Class J 4-6-2T No. 32326 (formerly *Bessborough*) and some Class I3 4-4-2Ts are joined by their successor, one of the very capable LMS design Fairburn 2-6-4Ts. The Class J would be withdrawn in June 1951, by which time many of the I3s had also disappeared, though that class did survive until 1952. By then the Fairburn tanks had been joined by their BR Standard 'clones'. Below, further transition is evident, this time in roofing styles, with a BR steel and asbestos covering which had replaced the twin pitches in 1955; coal stage pilot Class H No. 31162 watches Class U1 No. 31902 depart westwards on 24th May 1961. The shed closed just over four years later, but was retained, latterly housing one of BR's Emergency Control Trains until that was declared redundant. The building today stands empty, in the hope that it will once again house working steam, as the locomotive depot of the ambitious Tunbridge Wells & Eridge Railway Preservation Society.

S.C. Nash & T. Wright

Plate 301: The oldest engine shed of the LSWR system was that at **Wadebridge** on the isolated Bodmin & Wadebridge Railway, opened in 1834 and purchased by the LSWR 13 years later. For the next 48 years Wadebridge (and possibly another B&WR shed at Bodmin) was responsible for maintaining services, latterly using one or two motley LSWR engines that had to be delivered by sea. For example: 7th March 1874 to March 1886: ex-Engineer's Department 2-4-0T *Scott;* August 1885 to June 1895: Manning Wardle 0-6-0ST *Jumbo;* 24th May 1893 to June 1895: 2-4-0WT No. 248. From 1st June 1895, however, Wadebridge was finally attained by the LSWR's North Cornwall line and a new two-road engine shed brought into service. At that point the B&WR depot closed, to stand for many more years in alternative use, although the author is unaware of its final fate. This picture comes from an anonymous copy negative and shows Wadebridge B&WR engine shed, purportedly around 1915.

Author's collection

Plate 302: **Wadebridge's** 1895 shed is visible here from the west, c1935, showing the turntable and, flanking the depot, the water tank and sand house. This was the 'original' end of the building, which was extended in an easterly direction some 12 to 13 years after opening.

B. Matthews collection

Plate 303: The other end of **Wadebridge**, displaying the engine hoist installed with the 1907 extension. A coal stage was behind the camera – originally just an open platform, it was later fitted with a canopy to give protection from the Cornish elements. The depot closed in 1965, housed the odd diesel for a few years and was demolished in 1969.

B. Matthews collection

Plate 304: Glimpsed in the two preceding pictures, **Wadebridge's** allocation of Beattie 2-4-0WTs gave it legendary status, so we cannot leave the subject without featuring one of that trio of famous engines. Here is the odd man out – the only one with square splashers – No. 30586, inside Wadebridge shed on 25th May 1957. Also of interest are the dwarf brick walls and peeling woodwork above, the diagram board with an enthusiast trying to track down a missing engine, and the new smoke ducting. One wonders how many times that ducting was renewed during Wadebridge's 70 years of service to steam.

T. Wright

Plate 305: When **Waterloo** station opened in 1848 it was provided with a two-road locomotive shed – presumably to reduce the amount of light engine working to and from Nine Elms depot, over 1¹/₂ miles away. This contemporary engraving shows the shed standing on the viaduct, some way from the terminus building. As Waterloo grew though, the engine house was absorbed into the fabric of the station and finally disappeared in the large reconstruction scheme of the early 1900s.

NRM

WATERLOO STATION IN 1848.

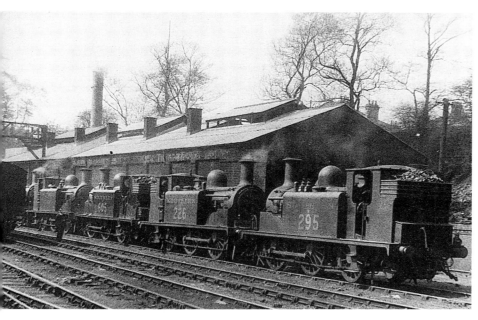

Plates 306 & 307: The original southern terminus of the London & Croydon Railway, **(West) Croydon's** engine shed opened on 1st June 1839 and by 1st May, five years later, ten engines were stationed there. Route extensions to Epsom, Wimbledon and Selhurst, between 1847 and 1865, led to the building being lengthened, despite its awkward site hard up against an embankment. That bank caused a problem during one of those famous Victorian blizzards when, on 17th January 1881, 0-4-4T No. 231 was trapped by drifting snow and could not work the first train up to London Bridge. Undeterred, the engine crew, shed lighter-up and some passengers dug a path for No. 231 which was then able to haul its diagrammed working – albeit a little late! Electrification reduced the depot's workings and Norwood Junction shed's opening in 1935 finally allowed closure and demolition. West Croydon is seen here above, on 17th April 1925 and below, about three years later, after repairs had altered the roof's outline. The limit of the c1865 extension is marked by the join in the roof above the fourth locomotive in the lower picture.

H.C. Casserley & Author's collection

Plate 308: Opened on 7th July 1881 and absorbed by the SER in the same year, the Westerham Valley Railway had the statutory one-road shed at its **Westerham** terminal. The branch was noteworthy for its long-term resident engines, which included Class Q 0-4-4T No. 366, Class O 0-6-0 No. 296 and Class 118 2-4-0 No. 17 or 252. Kitson steam railmotors were used during 1905/6, but were not a success due to their limited passenger space, so locomotives again stabled at Westerham until closure of the shed, at the relatively early date of 1925. This photograph, from around 1920, includes one of the very few known glimpses of the depot, in the distance, with the branch goods 0-6-0 in residence.

S.C. Nash collection

Plates 309 & 310: **Weymouth** LSWR shed came into use early in 1857 and stood opposite a two-road **GWR** broad gauge depot, with a shared dual-gauge turntable between. An outstation of Dorchester, the shed at Weymouth housed a couple of tank engines for shunting and local services over the Portland and Easton branch, first opened on 16th October 1865; it also gave succour to visiting main line engines of course. As such it survived for a remarkably long time, not being closed until January 1939, after which Southern locomotives used the GWR's second (1885) shed at Radipole. The LSWR depot is seen from the rear above, about 1905, with an LSWR train running into the station. An interesting fact, not previously appreciated, was that the first GWR shed still stood, some 20 years after being superseded – its roof and smoke vents are just visible, left of the water tank. At the bottom is an end-on view of the wooden LSWR building on 4th October 1931, with O2 No. 177 in residence, sporting a conical smokebox door. Notice too how the style of smoke vents had changed since 1905.

Author's collection & A.W. Croughton, courtesy J. Lucking

Plates 311 & 312: **Wimborne Junction** marked the joining of LSWR and Somerset & Dorset lines. Both companies shared a locomotive depot that by the latter 19th century comprised two buildings. These were one-road and two-road in layout, the former with a 45ft turntable outside and the latter in two sections, indicating an extension at some time. It appears the single-road building came first, in the early 1860s, but whether it was of LSWR or S&DR origin is not clear. The two-road shed appeared at an unknown date, but by 1909 was in such a state it had to be replaced, by the S&DJR, with a building of distinctly LSWR 'looks'. The single-road building disappeared at the same time, leaving the new depot to serve, for what turned out to be less than 14 years, as it closed in January 1923; at that time the LSWR allocation was four engines. Wimborne Junction's sheds were extremely rare photographic subjects and the only view so far located is at top, dating from around 1913. It shows the side of the 1909 building from the west; the S&D line to Bailey Gate passes beneath the camera. Below, we observe the filled-in pits and wall foundations around 1937; in the distance the original Southampton & Dorchester Railway main line passes from north to south (left to right).

B. Matthews collection & W.A. Camwell

Plate 313: **Winchester's** LSWR station had a goods yard large enough to justify provision of a full time shunting engine. Basic locomotive facilities had been available for some time before 1928, when the SR put up the corrugated iron shed distantly seen above, on 22nd July 1958. Notice the incongruous design, having doors at the front but a completely open rear! Class B4 0-4-0 tanks (No. 30089 was formerly named *Trouville*) were standard fare for many years, their short wheelbase being ideal for the sharply curved yard area. They gave way in October 1963 to Drewry 204hp diesel shunters that remained until Winchester Goods closed in 1969.

B. Hilton

Plate 314: The first temporary London & Southampton Railway terminus out of Nine Elms, Woking station and shed opened on 21st May 1838, with the line being extended by stages, through to Southampton, on 11th May 1840. **Woking** became a junction on 5th May 1845, with the line to Guildford and the shed thereafter housed one or two engines for shunting, trips, and main line pilot duties – the latter usually being drawn from Nine Elms' more run-down examples though! Typical residents were, 1866-70 'Minerva' class 2-4-0WTs Nos 16 *Salisbury* and 39 *Wizard;* June 1873 'Volcano' class 2-4-0 *Alecto;* mid-1880s Class 231 2-4-0 No. 236 and Class 415 4-4-2T No. 487; 1889-97 Class T1 0-4-4Ts Nos 71 and 74. Closure came apparently, about 1897, but this unique c1905 picture of T9 class No. 703 passing at speed with a 'down' express, clearly shows several engines around the one-road hipped roof depot. By 1914 though, the building had disappeared, leaving only a 50ft turntable and possibly a coal platform.

S.C. Nash collection

Plates 315 & 316: Yeovil was reached, from Salisbury on 1st June 1860, one month and eighteen days before the Exeter & Yeovil Railway opened throughout. The E&YR built a substantial three-road engine shed at **Yeovil (Town)** station, seen here from the same vantage point in 1928 (above) and on 19th July 1961 (centre). Already gone by 1928, was the depot's original turntable; engine No. 293 stands on its site. Later changes, in the 33 years 1928-1961, were that the station lost its marvellous overall roof and there was a definite come-down in locomotive quantity and, arguably, 'appeal'. Also the engine shed's roof had been modified and the covered coal stage has given way to a steam crane (2 ton, Grafton-built, No. DS453). One Bulleid Pacific may be identified in the lower view: No. 34081 *92 Squadron.*

Author's collection & G. Coltas

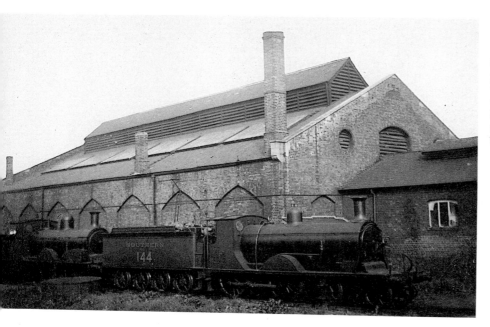

Plate 317: An aspect of **Yeovil** shed rarely photographed – the rear of the depot on 18th August 1938, with a 'Jubilee' class 0-4-2 and Class K10 No. 144 temporarily put out to grass. The pictures on this page will give the reader a very good idea of what the elusive E&YR shed at Exeter Queen Street (*Plates 99 & 100*) looked like – except that that was a through building, as opposed to Yeovil's being single-ended.

J. Lucking

Acknowledgements

As with my book on GWR sheds, the most satisfying words to write are those which publicly say thank you to the many people whose willing help made it all possible. Like GWR, they are listed below but first, a few names must receive special mention and foremost among them is Sid Nash. Almost one in six of all pictures are of his taking, or from his incredible collection, and as for the historical information – well! Suffice it to say that without Sid this book could never have been.

Next comes that ace detective of old photographs, Bernard Matthews, who once again allowed me to plunder his files, invariably through the hazy "mists" of the Glen Livet! Fourth, and equally important, has been the contribution of Mr H.C. Casserley, that doyen of shed photographers and a person to whom all railway enthusiasts should forever be grateful. Last, but not least, comes the National Railway Museum, and the special help given by John Edgington, particularly for the use of some of his own superb pictures.

For reference, I consulted a number of works, in particular *An Historical Survey of Southern Sheds* by Chris Hawkins and George Reeve (OPC 1979), from which many details were gleaned. Great credit must go to Chris and George for tracing many of the older sheds listed in this album. Much resort was also made to the late Don Bradley's encyclopaedic studies of the locomotives of the LBSCR, LCDR, LSWR, SER and SECR, all published by the Railway Correspondence and Travel Society. Next, *A Regional History of the Railways of Great Britain, Volume 2, Southern England* by H.P. White (David & Charles 1982), provided much useful data, as did numerous 'dips' into the RCTS *Railway Observer,* the *Railway Magazine, Railway World* and a number of private individuals' note books and reminiscences. Finally come a few words of tribute to Britain's library and museum services – their responses to my usually obscure, long-distance enquiries were invariably swift and comprehensive.

The new management of OPC, particularly Peter Nicholson, deserve praise for their help and continued toleration of my operating so far from the editorial base, and a special mention must also be made of the Engine Shed Society. Many of those named on this page are members, with myself, of the ESS and I am very grateful to the Society's journal *Link* and Chairman Nick Pigott for much assistance rendered.

But, above all comes my family. My loving thanks again go to Jane, who amazingly still hasn't divorced me, and to Carl and Simon. This album is especially for my two sons, for all the times I didn't play with them because daddy was "doing the book". My deepest gratitude to you all.

The Photographers

British Rail
Colin Caddy
Bill Camwell
Gordon Coltas
Tim Cooper
C.H. Eden
Bruce Ellis (A.G. Ellis colln.)
Ken Fairey
Barry Fletcher
E.V. Fry
H. Garratt
Dr. Terry Gough
A.R. Goult
Brian Green
Norman Hamshere
Brian Hilton
Lens of Sutton

Locomotive Club of Great Britain (Ken Nunn colln.)
John Lucking
Brian Morrison
Terry Nicholls
Cedric Owen
Norman Preedy
Royal Air Force Museum
Allan Sommerfield
John Spence
Neil Sprinks
Bill Stubbs
Peter Tatlow
D. Wallis & Mrs M. Mason (the late E. Wallis colln.)
West Sussex County Council
Derek Winkworth
Tony Wright

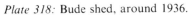

Plate 318: Bude shed, around 1936.   B. Matthews